NOSH
FOR STUDENTS

BY JOY MAY
& THE FAMILY TEAM

OTHER BOOKS IN THE NOSH SERIES BY JOY MAY

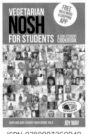

ISBN: 9780993260940

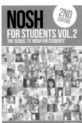

ISBN: 9780956746405

ISBN: 9780956746436

ISBN: 9780956746481

ISBN: 9780993260957

ISBN: 9780993260971

ISBN: 9780993260964

ISBN: 9780993260902

ISBN: 9780956746498

ISBN: 9780993260919

@NOSHBOOKS

WE WOULD LOVE TO HEAR FROM YOU. USE
#NOSHBOOKS

CONTENTS

THIS ALL STARTED WITH BEN...

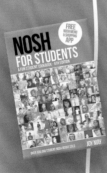

This is Ben, my son, going off to university. He never learned how to cook before going to uni, so after a whole semester eating pizza and Mars bars, he looked dinstinctly lethargic and pale!

Ben used to call me from uni, asking basic questions, that, to him, were major roadblocks to cooking. It was just too easy to pop a pizza in the oven, or get a take-away. Something needed to change.

I tried writing recipe cards, but they didn't work. He had no idea what the food should look like at the end. He needed something more visual.

I decided, therefore, to write NOSH FOR STUDENTS, include a photo with every recipe and also make everything as straightforward as possible. Since the first edition, I have been able to help Ben, and around **half a million other students,** get cooking.

I wrote this book for Ben, and also for the many students who head off to uni each year. It's a huge step for most, so I hope this book helps you stay happy and healthy in your new life away from home. Maybe you'll even start to enjoy cooking. You never know!

No need for weighing scales. What student kitchen has got a set of those?!

Just grab a mug and get cooking. Cooking isn't about perfection, it's about getting tasty food on the table.

Throughout the book I have used a mug to measure ingredients. The mug holds 1/2 a pint (300ml) of liquid and is the size of the mug pictured opposite.

A MUG :

ACTUAL SIZE

ALL YOU NEED

FOR LINKS TO ALL OF THESE GO TO:
noshbooks.com/allyouneed

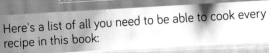

Here's a list of all you need to be able to cook every recipe in this book:

- ☑ MUG (APPROX 1/2 PINT)
- ☑ TABLESPOON, ONE YOU SERVE WITH
- ☑ DESSERTSPOON, ONE YOU EAT CEREAL WITH
- ☑ TEASPOON, ONE YOU STIR TEA WITH
- ☑ WOODEN SPOON
- ☑ CHOPPING BOARD
- ☑ SHARP KNIFE
- ☑ FISH SLICE
- ☑ COLANDER
- ☑ MIXING BOWL
- ☑ CHEESE GRATER
- ☑ SMALL AND MEDIUM SAUCEPAN, WITH LIDS
- ☑ SHALLOW CASSEROLE DISH, WITH LID
  - ☑ NON-STICK BAKING TRAY
    - ☑ 2 X CAKE TINS (23CM)
      - ☑ LOAF TIN
        - ☑ MUFFIN TRAY
          - ☑ FRYING PAN
            - ☑ WOK

10 TIPS TO SAVE MONEY ON FOOD

SCAN ME

1 **Plan** a weekly menu and create a shopping list.

2 _Never_ shop hungry.

3 Downshift to **value brands** (ditch the brands).

4 Set a **weekly budget**, and stick to it.

5 **Bulk-buy** the basics with flatmates.

6 **Learn the difference** between "best before" and "use-by".

7 **Take your own lunches** when you go into uni.

8 **Bulk-cook** with flatmates.

9 Look for supermarkets that offer **student discounts.**

10 **Freeze,** in portions, everything that is freezable.

PLAN, PLAN, PLAN

Food-buying trends are changing. Research shows that the traditional 'weekly shop' is falling out of fashion, in favour of popping to the shops 3-4 times a week, as and when you need it. Whilst that gives you certain level of flexibility, there are downsides. It's just too easy to choose convenience foods, or the same things over and over again.

If you plan your meals for the coming week, or at least a few days ahead, and shop for it, you are much more likely to actually cook it. Nobody likes to waste good food! Try planning your meals for a while and see the difference it makes.

Remember to think about all of your meals, including breakfast and lunch. If you don't plan for them, you will end up having to snack at uni, which will cost a fortune.

Buck the trend. While everyone else is ditching the old school, 'weekly shop', why not embrace it.

#BRINGBACKTHEBIGTROLLEY

YOUR FREE NOSH BOOKS APP

To help you plan and shop for your food, we have designed a FREE app to create menus and shopping lists. Simply browse any of our books and add recipes of your choice to a weekly menu. The app does all the tedious work of creating the shopping list for you and boom! You're ready to shop.

No more aimless wandering around the supermarket, only to get home and still not be able to make a meal. What have you got to lose?

Download it for FREE.

SCAN ME

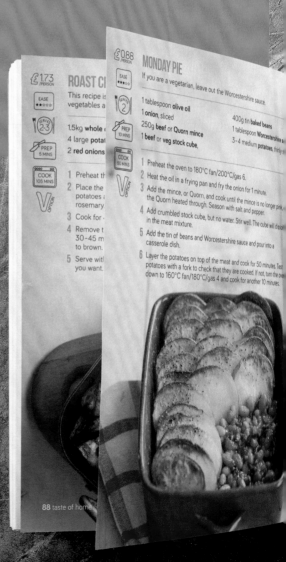

Recipe card: **ROAST C...** £1.73 /PERSON · EASE · SERVES 2-3 · PREP 5 MINS · COOK 105 MINS · V OPTION

This recipe is... vegetables a...

1.5kg **whole**...
4 large **potat**...
2 **red onions**...

1 Preheat th...
2 Place the... potatoes a... rosemary...
3 Cook for...
4 Remove t... 30-45 m... to brown.
5 Serve with... you want.

Recipe card: **MONDAY PIE** £0.88 /PERSON · EASE · SERVES 2

If you are a vegetarian, leave out the Worcestershire sauce.

1 tablespoon **olive oil**
1 **onion**, sliced
250g **beef** or **Quorn** mince
1 **beef** or **veg stock cube**,
400g tin **baked beans**
1 tablespoon **Worcestershire s**...
3-4 medium **potatoes**, thinly s...

1 Preheat the oven to 180°C fan/200°C/gas 6.
2 Heat the oil in a frying pan and fry the onion for 1 minute.
3 Add the mince, or Quorn, and cook until the mince is no longer pink, ... the Quorn heated through. Season with salt and pepper.
4 Add crumbled stock cube, but no water. Stir well. The cube will dissolv... in the meat mixture.
5 Add the tin of beans and Worcestershire sauce and pour into a casserole dish.
6 Layer the potatoes on top of the meat and cook for 50 minutes. Test ... potatoes with a fork to check that they are cooked. If not, turn the ove... down to 160°C fan/180°C/gas 4 and cook for another 10 minutes.

88 taste of home

STORECUPBOARD & FRIDGE

Here are some basics to keep in your storecupboard and fridge. In student halls, or shared houses, you will usually have a shelf in the fridge, one drawer in the freezer, and a cupboard to yourself.

FRIDGE/FREEZER

- spare loaf of bread in freezer
- butter/spread
- milk
- eggs
- cheese
- mayo
- curry paste

STORECUPBOARD

- rice
- pasta
- cereal
- tinned chopped tomatoes
- baked beans
- Worcestershire sauce
- pilau rice seasoning
- soy sauce
- olive oil

- salt and pepper
- stock cubes
- sugar
- flour

USEFUL HERBS AND SPICES
- mixed dried herbs
- dried basil
- chilli flakes
- paprika

HOW LONG CAN I KEEP THIS BEFORE IT KILLS ME?

Raw meat	1 day in the fridge.
Bacon	2 to 3 days in the fridge.
Cooked meat: cooked chicken/ ham, etc.	3 days maximum in the fridge.
Eggs	1 month from lay date (usually the use-by date on the egg).
Milk	2–3 days once opened. If unopened, see 'best-before' date.
Butter and margarine	6 weeks
Cheese	1 week once opened, 2 weeks unopened. Keep cheese wrapped.
Onions and potatoes	1 week, best out of the fridge and in a cool dark place.
Green vegetables	1 week in fridge.
Carrots, parsnips, etc.	1 week in fridge.
Salad, lettuce, cucumber, tomatoes, peppers, etc.	1 week in fridge.
Leftovers	ONLY the day after the food has been cooked. All kinds of nasties can begin to lurk there!

HOW CAN I TELL IF SOMETHING IS PAST IT?

Learn the difference between 'best-before' and 'use-by' dates:
'Best-before' dates are about food quality, not food safety. You can eat things that are past their best-before dates, they just might not taste as good as they should.

'Use-by dates' are about food safety. Consume up to that date, but not after.

Here are some 'red flag' signs when the best place for your food is the bin.

Cheese	Green mould on the surface.
Potatoes	Skin is turning green and soft with excessive 'eyes'.
Yogurts	Lid 'puffing up'. If opened, the smell changes and it tastes 'sharp'.
Bread	Mould around the crust.
Vegetables	Originally crisp, vegetables, now soft and soggy, e.g. 'bendy' carrots.
Raw meat	Colour changes to brown or khaki colour.
Chicken	Begins to smell bad

REHEATING & STORING

REHEAT FOOD THOROUGHLY. It should be 'piping hot'. This means all the food should be steaming and you will need to use a cloth to handle the plate from the microwave.

COVER YOUR FOOD WITH CLING FILM AND PLACE ON A HIGH HEAT for approximately 2½ mins in a 700 watt microwave. However, refer to point above if you are unsure.

AVOID REHEATING PORK OR SHELLFISH.

KEEP THINGS COVERED IN THE FRIDGE This helps things last longer and rules out cross-contamination. Important if you share a fridge with someone who leaves disgusting things in there! If you cook a meal one day, eat any leftovers the next day, but not after that.

BE VERY CAREFUL WITH RICE
Cool it quickly and place it in the fridge. Don't leave it in the pan to cool down, as that will take too long. Reheat thoroughly.

DON'T KEEP OPENED TINS IN THE FRIDGE
Once a tin is open to the air, a chemical reaction occurs, affecting the food. Transfer any excess to a bowl and cover with cling film.

7 STEPS TO SUCCESS

1 **Start simple.** Use our 'difficulty rating' to choose simple meals if you are not yet a confident cook. Don't run before you can walk. Build in confidence first.

2 **Read the recipe** all the way through before you begin cooking. Get a clear idea of everything you are going to be doing. Avoid surprises!

3 **Prepare all your ingredients** before you begin to cook. For example, don't try to chop vegetables whilst you are frying things. Nobody needs that stress!

4 **Try to keep things clean.** If you are all prepped and ready to start, have a quick clear up before you begin. It will make cooking much more enjoyable.

5 **Avoid trying something new** when you are cooking for others, unless they are going to help. If they help, that's where you can really have fun!

6 **Avoid having your hob too high.** There are no prizes for finishing first. Chill out and avoid burning things.

7 **Season and taste your food** as you go. Seasoning whilst cooking is better than when it is on your plate.

WHAT DO I DO IF...

...everything I cook in the oven is burnt or undercooked?

It could be that, if you have an older oven, the thermostat is not working quite as well as it should. Don't give up, just adjust by raising or lowering the temperature you set and make a note of what works. Also, temperatures in some ovens vary, depending on which shelf you use. Where possible, use middle shelves. Check what kind of oven you have - Centigrade fan oven, Centigrade, or gas mark- then set the temperature specified on the recipe.

...I don't have a microwave to defrost food?

Keep the food wrapped up and place in cold water. Don't use hot water. The best thing is to plan ahead, take food out of the freezer, and leave in the fridge overnight to defrost.

...everything I cook on my hob is burnt?

Either you need to keep the heat turned down, or just keep an eye on things and keep them moving. No going off to ring your mates whilst trying to cook.

...I don't have a lid for my casserole dish?

Cover the dish with tin foil.

...I have made things too spicy?

With Chilli Con Carne, just try adding another tin of tomatoes. With a curry, peel and cut a potato into four and add to the curry. Simmer for 10 minutes and remove the potato.

...I don't have a pastry brush?

Use your fingers, or a spoon.

BOILING VEGGIES

Generally, most vegetables need to be cooked in just enough water to cover them.

1 Bring the water to the boil.
2 Once boiling, add the vegetables and a little salt, and simmer gently with the lid on the pan. If you keep the source of the heat low, you will preserve a little more of the nutrition in the vegetables.

Swedes and turnips	3cm chunks	20–25 mins
Potatoes	3cm chunks	10–15 mins
Parsnips, carrots	cut into 2cm rings	10–15 mins
Cauliflower	broken into little trees	5–7 mins
Broccoli	broken into little trees	5–7 mins
Green beans	cut off the stalk and tail	5 mins
Cabbage	cut into long thin strips	5 mins
Sugar snaps	leave as they are	2 mins
Mangetout	leave as they are	1 min

Note:
For **spinach**, cook just enough to make the leaves wilt. You will only need a quarter of a mug of water in the bottom of the pan.

For **cabbage**, use half a mug of water in the pan, drain after cooking and add some butter and black pepper. Return to the pan and cook for another 2 minutes to dry the cabbage a little.

ROASTING VEGGIES

1 Preheat the oven to 180°C fan/200°C/gas 6.

2 Put the vegetables on a flat roasting/baking tray and sprinkle them with salt and olive oil. Turn them over with your hands to make sure that the oil is covering all the pieces. Set them on the tray with flat sides up. If the flat sides are on the tray itself, they will tend to stick. Sprinkle with rosemary if you wish.

3 Put in the middle of the oven for 30 minutes. Check to see if any are getting too brown, maybe the ones around the edge. Move, or turn over as necessary. Put back in the oven for another 20 minutes. You can put a mix of veg in (see photo below). If you are roasting individual veg, see timings below:

Potatoes	cut into 5cm chunks	40–50 mins
Butternut squash	peel, cut into 5cm chunks	30–40 mins
Parsnips	cut into 4, lengthways	40–45 mins
Sweet potatoes	peel, cut into 5cm chunks	40–50 mins
Onions	cut into 6 wedges	40–50 mins
Fennel	cut into 4 wedges	30–40 mins
Tomatoes	cut the skin	20–25 mins
Peppers	remove seeds and stalk, cut into large pieces	25 mins

PERFECT RICE EVERY TIME

There are many different types of rice you can buy. I recommend using basmati. It is slightly more expensive than some types, but has a much better flavour and texture.

$$\frac{1}{2} \text{ MUG RICE} \quad + \quad \text{1 MUG WATER} \quad = \quad \text{RICE FOR 1 PERSON}$$

(plus 1 teaspoon of pilau rice seasoning, optional)

1 Using a pan with a lid, bring the water to the boil, add the pilau rice seasoning, if you are using it, and stir until it has dissolved.

2 Add the rice and stir once. Bring back to the boil. Once boiling, turn down the heat to very low, so that the rice simmers gently. Put the lid on the pan and cook for approximately 10 minutes. Do not stir whilst the rice is cooking, or you will make it sticky. The rice should be cooked once the water has disappeared. Check occasionally to see if the water has boiled away.

3 Test the rice once the water has boiled away. If the rice is still too crunchy and the water has all gone, then you have boiled it too quickly. Add a little more water, replace the lid and cook for another 5 minutes.

SCAN ME

Joy did a video to show you how

HOW TO COOK PASTA

There are innumerable kinds of pasta made from different ingredients. Most will have instructions on the packets as to how to cook them. Just in case you have lost the packet, here are some general guidelines:

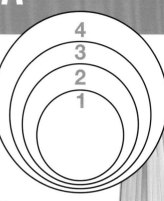

SPAGHETTI

1 Use the guide above to measure the quantities required for 1–4 people. Boil sufficient water in a pan to easily cover the spaghetti whilst cooking. Season with salt.

2 Once the salted water is boiling, lower the spaghetti sticks into the water. Once the half that is in the water has softened slightly, push the other half in. Simmer for 6–8 minutes.

3 Test one piece to see if it is cooked. Drain the water off and add one teaspoon of butter, or olive oil. Mix around to stop the spaghetti sticking together.

MOST OTHER PASTAS

Again, boil enough salted water to cover the pasta. Once the water is boiling, add the pasta. **One mug of dried pasta is plenty for one person with a very healthy appetite.** Simmer for the appropriate time. Drain and add butter, or olive oil, to prevent the pasta sticking together.

HERE IS A GUIDE, BUT IT STILL DEPENDS ON THE THICKNESS OF THE PASTA:

Tagliatelle	the stuff that comes in little nests. 4–5 minutes.
Spaghetti	6 minutes, depending how thick the spaghetti is.
Radiatore	looks like little radiators. 10 minutes.
Fusilli	little twists. 6–8 minutes.
Penne	little tubes, vary in size. 10–12 minutes..
Conchiglie	little shells. 6–8 minutes.
Macaroni	tiny tubes 12–15 minutes.
Farfalle	looks like little bows. 6–8 minutes.

JACKET POTATOES

Use medium or large potatoes. Always slice a cross in the skin with a knife before baking, or it may explode in the oven, or microwave. You will only get the crisp jackets if you cook the potatoes in the oven.

OVEN BAKED — Preheat the oven to 200°C fan/220°C/gas 7. Rub the skin with a little olive oil, sprinkle with salt, and bake for 50–60 minutes.

MICROWAVE AND OVEN — Preheat the oven to 200°C fan/220°C/gas 7. Cook in the microwave, on full power, for 5 minutes and then in the oven for 30 minutes.

MICROWAVE — 7–10 minutes on full power.

FILLINGS

When the potato is cooked, cut it open and add a little butter, then add any of the following suggestions:

THE SIMPLEST
Baked beans and/or grated cheese.

TUNA SWEETCORN AND MAYO
Mix together 1/2 x 185g tin of tuna with 1 tablespoon of mayo and 200g tin sweetcorn. Season well. (If you double these quantities, you will have some sandwich filling for the next day.)

COTTAGE CHEESE
1/2 x 250g tub of cottage cheese, mixed with 3 chopped spring onions and 12 defrosted, cooked prawns. You could add a chopped tomato if you wish. (Use the rest of the tub of cottage cheese in sandwiches.)

COOKED CHICKEN AND MAYO
If you have roasted a chicken (see p88), chop up a portion of it and add 1 tablespoon of mayo + 1/2 teaspoon mustard. Season with salt and pepper.

SMOKED MACKEREL
You can buy this quite cheaply. It is already cooked and in sealed bags. Take the skin off one piece and gently break up the fish. Add 2 chopped spring onions and 1 tablespoon of mayo, or crème fraîche. Season with salt and pepper. (Keep the rest of the fish covered in cling film and use in Smoked Mackerel Pasta Salad, see p52.)

CRISPY BACON AND HARD-BOILED EGGS
Hard boil 2 eggs (see p28), take off the shells and chop them up. Grill 2 rashers of streaky bacon and chop them up also. Mix together. You can add 1 tablespoon of mayo and/or a 200g tin of sweetcorn if you wish. Season with salt and pepper. (If you want to make a dish using bacon, e.g. Salsa Salad, p49, then just keep a couple of rashers for this recipe.)

INTERESTING SANDWICHES

Sandwiches don't have to be boring. Here are a few different, (and in some cases slightly odd) alternative, sandwich fillings compared with the normal 'ham and cheese' variety. Another way to make sandwiches more interesting is to vary the bread you use. Try to avoid white bread all the time, as too much of it is not good for you. Choose different kinds of wholemeal, granary loaves, bread buns or pitta breads.

BACON AND BANANA
Fry 3 slices of streaky bacon, until crisp. Whilst still hot, put in the sandwich with a sliced banana.

COTTAGE CHEESE WITH TOMATOES OR CUCUMBER
Chop a tomato, or a 4cm piece of cucumber, quite small. Mix together with $1/2$ x 250g pot of cottage cheese. Season well.

EGG MAYO
Hard boil 2 eggs (see p28). Rinse them under cold water, take off the shells and chop them up with a knife. Mix them together with 1 tablespoon of mayo and season with salt and pepper.

TUNA WITH HARD-BOILED EGGS
Drain a 185g tin of tuna and put half in a bowl. Hard boil 2 eggs (see p28), peel and chop and add to the bowl. Chop 2 spring onions and add to the bowl with 1 tablespoon of mayo. Mix together and season well.

PEANUT BUTTER AND BANANA
Spread a liberal amount of peanut butter on one slice. Spread jam, or honey, on top. Slice a banana and pile it in.

BLT
Fry 3 rashers of streaky bacon until crisp. Spread one slice of bread with mayo. Add 2 lettuce leaves and one sliced tomato. Season with pepper - the bacon has enough saltiness. Add the bacon on top.

COTTAGE CHEESE WITH BANANA
Spread the bread with a liberal amount of honey or jam. Top with cottage cheese. Slice a banana and pile into the sandwich.

CHICKEN AND MAYO WITH LETTUCE
If you have roasted a chicken and have some spare, cut it into small pieces. Spread mayo over one slice of bread and add the lettuce. Season with salt and pepper. Add the chicken on top.

SCRAMBLED EGGS, CHEESE AND TOMATO
Grate $1/2$ a mug of cheese. Chop a tomato quite finely. Heat a little butter in a small, non-stick saucepan, add the tomatoes and fry for 1 minute. Add 2 eggs and cook until they begin to set. Add the cheese and cook for 30 seconds. Season well and make the sandwich whilst the eggs are still hot.

STUFF ON TOAST

CHEESE ON TOAST

with a little something extra.

1 Preheat the grill and very lightly toast the bread.

2 Butter the toast. At this stage you can add things to go under the cheese, such as ham, pickle, Marmite, or sliced tomatoes.

3 Slice, or grate, the cheese and place on top. Make sure the cheese covers the edges of the toast to protect the corners of the bread from burning.

4 Place under the grill and cook until the cheese begins to bubble.

EGGIE BREAD

1 Break an egg into a mug and beat with a fork. Pour out onto a plate.

2 Dip one side of a thick slice of bread into the egg, quickly turn over and let the other side soak up the rest of the egg.

3 Put a 2cm cube of butter in a frying pan and heat gently, until the butter starts to bubble.

4 Add the bread and cook, turning over to brown both sides.

5 Serve with beans, HP or tomato sauce. To make it into breakfast, serve with honey, or maple syrup, and sliced fruit.

BEANS ON TOAST WITH EGG ON TOP

Toast the bread, heat the beans, and then fry or poach the eggs (see p28). Great with HP sauce.

GARLIC BREAD

This works best with medium-sized baguettes.

1 Finely chop 1 clove of garlic, and mix together with about 25g butter (measure using packet). You could add 1 teaspoon of dried chives at this point, if you wish.

2 Make diagonal cuts in the baguette, but not quite all the way through.

3 Push the garlic butter into the cuts.

4 Wrap the baguette in foil and bake in the oven for 10 minutes (200°C fan/220°C/gas 7).

WELSH RAREBIT

1/2 mug grated **Cheddar cheese**

2 teaspoons **flour**

1/2 mug **milk**

1/2 teaspoon **mustard**

1 teaspoon **Worcestershire Sauce**

1 **egg yolk**

25g **butter**, measure using packet

1 Without the heat on, put the grated cheese and flour in a small saucepan and mix well.

2 Add the rest of the ingredients and mix well.

3 Heat slowly until the mixture thickens and is hot. Serve on a thick slice of toast.

EGGS

BOIL

1. Using a small pan, fill ⅔ full with water and bring to the boil.
2. Lower the egg gently into the pan on a spoon.
3. Simmer briskly for 3 minutes for a very runny egg, 5 minutes and you will still be able to dip your 'soldiers' in the runny yolk, 12 minutes and it will be hard-boiled.

POACH

1. Using a small pan, or frying pan, half fill with water and add a good pinch of salt. Bring to the boil, then turn down, until the water is only just moving.
2. Break the egg into a mug, or cup, and gently pour into the water. Do not stir or turn the heat up, just let it cook gently. It will take 2–4 minutes, depending on the size of the egg.
3. Once the egg has gone opaque, gently lift out with a fish slice and let the water drain from it.

FRY

1. Heat 2 teaspoons of butter in the frying pan, until the butter just bubbles.
2. Break the egg into a mug and then gently pour into the frying pan.
3. Cook on a medium/low heat, until the egg is set.
4. Using a fish slice, turn the egg over half-way through cooking, if you want 'easy-over', hard yolk.

SCRAMBLE

1. Using a small milk pan, preferably non-stick, add a 25g butter (measure using packet) and heat gently until the butter bubbles.
2. Break the egg into the pan. Stir slowly, breaking up the egg yolk.
3. When the egg is almost set, take off the heat. The egg will continue to cook in its own heat. If you cook it too long, it will become rubbery. Season with salt and pepper.
4. You can add grated cheese and/or chopped tomatoes half-way through the cooking.

SCAN ME

Some people struggle with poaching eggs, so Joy did a video. Check it out

OMELETTES

FOR 1 PERSON

1 Put two or three eggs in a mug and beat well with a fork, adding two tablespoons of water. Season with salt and pepper.

2 Preheat the grill.

3 Melt about a dessertspoon of butter in the frying pan. Once it begins to 'bubble', pour the egg mixture into the pan.

4 As the egg begins to set on the bottom of the pan, gently move the set egg with a fish slice and allow the runny egg to take its place. Do this with two or three sweeping movements; don't stir, or you will get 'scrambled egg'. If you are making double the quantity, repeat this process once more.

5 While there is still a little runny egg on the top, take off the heat, add whatever filling you want, top with cheese (not essential) and place the frying pan under the hot grill. The omelette should rise. Once it is browned on the top, remove from the grill and turn out onto a plate. Serve with salad or garlic bread.

Suggested fillings – cheese, tomato, mushrooms, fried onions, crispy grilled bacon cut into pieces, cooked chicken, ham or any combination of these ingredients.

SAUCES

PEPPER SAUCE You can **use stirred into cooked pasta.**

1 tablespoon **olive oil**	1 clove **garlic**, chopped
1¹/2 **red peppers**, chopped	1 tablespoon **cream**
¹/2 **onion**, sliced	¹/2 teaspoon **sugar**

1 Heat the oil in a saucepan and fry the peppers, onions and garlic, over a medium heat for 5 minutes, until they are really soft.

2 Add the sugar and cream and mix. Season with salt and pepper.

3 Blitz with a hand-held blender, if you have one, or use as it is.

QUICK CHEESE SAUCE

This is a simple and versatile **basic sauce**. You can use this sauce as a pasta sauce, **for veggie bakes, lasagne** and **cauliflower cheese.**

1 mug grated **Cheddar cheese**	¹/8 teaspoon **paprika**
1 tablespoon **flour**	1 mug **milk**
salt and **pepper**	25g **butter**, measure using packet

1 Without the heat on, put the grated cheese, flour, salt, pepper and paprika into a saucepan, and stir well.

2 Add the milk and butter. Put on a low heat and bring to the boil, stirring all the time. The sauce should thicken.

PIQUANT TOMATO SAUCE You can **use stirred into cooked pasta**.

1 tablespoon **olive oil**	1 tablespoon **tomato purée**
1 **onion**, sliced	1 tablespoon **white wine vinegar**
400g tin **chopped tomatoes**	1 teaspoon **sugar**
1 teaspoon **black pepper**	

1 Heat the oil in a saucepan and fry the onions until they become soft.

2 Add the rest of the ingredients and bring to the boil. Simmer for 2–3 minutes.

3 Blitz with a hand-held blender, if you have one, or use as it is.

BAGELS

CREAM CHEESE AND AVOCADO

2 tablespoons **Philadelphia cream cheese**

½ **avocado**, sliced

1 **spring onion**, sliced

½ teaspoon freshly chopped **dill** (optional)

1 Toast the bagels and spread with butter. Add the toppings.

TURKEY AND CRANBERRY SAUCE

2 slices **cooked turkey**

4 teaspoons **cranberry sauce**

¼ mug grated **Cheddar cheese**

1 Toast the bagels and spread with butter. Add the toppings and put under the grill until the cheese bubbles.

SALT BEEF

2 slices **salt beef**

2 **gherkins**, sliced

1 teaspoon **mustard**

1 Toast the bagels and spread with butter. Add the toppings.

PEPPERONI AND JALEPEÑO EGG

¼ mug grated **Cheddar cheese**

8 slices **pepperoni**

2 **eggs**

2 **jalepeño peppers**, sliced

1 Put the cheese and pepperoni on the bagel and put under the grill until the cheese bubbles.

2 Fry the egg with the sliced jalepeños on top.

FAST FOOD

Home from uni and in a rush to get out? Here are some quick and easy things for you to try.

CAJUN CHICKEN ALFREDO

Traditional Alfredos are basically cream and garlic with chicken, but adding the cajun spices really lifts this dish to another level.

£1.80 /PERSON

EASE
★★☆☆☆

SERVES
2

PREP
20 MINS

---

linguine (see p21)

2 **chicken breasts**

2 teaspoons **Cajun seasoning**

2 tablespoons **olive oil**

6 **spring onions**, chopped

1 clove **garlic**, finely chopped

1/2 mug (150ml) **double cream**

2 teaspoons **dried basil**

juice of 1/2 **lemon**

---

1 Cook the linguine in the same way you would cook linguine (see p21). Drain and return to the pan.

2 Meanwhile, toss the chicken breast in the Cajun seasoning.

3 Heat the oil in a frying pan and fry the chicken, on a medium heat, for 2 minutes each side. Turn down the heat and fry for a further 3–4 minutes each side with a lid on the pan. Remove from the pan and set to one side.

4 Add the onions and garlic to the pan and fry for 30 seconds.

5 Add the cream, basil and lemon, season with salt and pepper, and cook for a minute. Add the cooked linguine and gently mix.

6 Slice the chicken into strips and serve on top of the pasta.

£0.84 /PERSON

EASE
★★☆☆☆

SERVES 4

PREP 15 MINS

COOK 25 MINS

V OPTION

BEEFY MINCE AND PASTA BAKE

Very simple to make and share with flatmates. It is OK reheated in the microwave, but best eaten straight away.

1¹/₂ mugs **pasta** (we used fusilli)

1 tablespoon **olive oil**

1 **onion**, chopped

2 cloves **garlic**, finely chopped

500g **beef** or **Quorn mince**

1 **beef** or **veg stock cube**

295g tin **Campbell's condensed tomato soup** (undiluted)

1 teaspoon **dried basil**

¹/₂ mug grated **Cheddar cheese**

1 Preheat the oven to 200°C fan/220°C/gas 7.

2 Put the pasta on to cook (see p21).

3 Heat the oil in a frying pan or wok. Fry the onion and garlic until soft.

4 Add the mince and cook until no longer pink.

5 Add the stock cube, tomato soup, herbs and some salt and pepper.

6 Drain the pasta well and add to the meat mixture. Transfer to a casserole dish.

7 Top with grated cheese and cook for 20–25 minutes. The top should be browned.

LEMONY COUSCOUS CHICKEN

£2.57 /PERSON

EASE
★★☆☆☆

SERVES 2

PREP 25 MINS

V OPTION

If you have roasted a chicken, you could use any leftovers in this recipe. Add at stage 3, but you will only need to heat it for 30 seconds at that stage, then go on to the next stages. It should be thoroughly heated by stage 6.

1 mug **couscous**

rind of 1 **lemon**, finely grated + the juice of half a **lemon**

2 mugs **boiling water**

50g **butter**, measure using packet

1 **onion**, thinly sliced

1 **red pepper**, diced

1 clove **garlic**, finely chopped

1 large **chicken breast**, cut into small pieces or 150g **Quorn pieces**

6 **mushrooms**, sliced

½ x 100g pack **pine nuts**

1 **fat red chilli**, thinly sliced

1 teaspoon **dried chives**

1 Place the couscous, lemon rind and juice in a bowl. Pour the 2 mugs of boiling water over it. Stir, cover with a plate or cling film, and leave to stand for about 5 minutes.

2 Heat the butter in a pan and add the onions, peppers and garlic. Fry until the onions are soft. Season with salt and pepper.

3 Add the chicken pieces and cook until they are no longer pink.

4 Add the mushrooms and cook for 1 minute.

5 Add the pine nuts and the chilli. Just allow to heat through.

6 Stir in the couscous and chives.

£ 1.25 /PERSON

EASE
★★☆☆☆

SERVES 2

PREP 15 MINS

COOK 20 MINS

V OPTION

CHICKEN RISOTTO

This is a good way to stretch one chicken breast to make enough for two people.

25g **butter**, measure using packet

1 **onion**, chopped

1 **chicken breast**, cut into bite-size pieces or 100g **Quorn pieces**

4 **mushrooms**, sliced

½ **red pepper**, chopped

⅓ mug **rice**, can be risotto or basmati

½ **chicken** or **veg stock cube**, crumbled

½ teaspoon **curry paste**

1 mug **water**

1 teaspoon **dried chives**

200g tin **sweetcorn**, drained

1 Heat the butter in a frying pan and fry the onion until soft.

2 Add the chicken and fry until the outside is no longer pink. Season with salt and pepper.

3 Add the mushroom, pepper, rice (uncooked), stock cube, curry paste, water and chives. Simmer gently for 20 minutes, stirring from time to time. Add more water if the mixture has dried up before the rice is cooked. There should be very little liquid left when the dish is finished.

4 Add the sweetcorn and heat through and serve.

CREAMY CHICKEN

This is such a simple dish, you will find yourself coming back to it again and again. It is easy to scale-up if you are cooking for more people.

£1.77 /PERSON

EASE
★☆☆☆☆

SERVES
2

PREP
15 MINS

V OPTION

1 mug **basmati rice**

1 teaspoon **pilau rice seasoning** (optional)

1 tablespoon **olive oil**

1 **onion**, sliced

1 clove **garlic**, finely chopped

2 **chicken breasts**, cut into pieces or 200g **Quorn pieces**

5-6 **mushrooms**, sliced

1/2 mug (150ml) **double cream**

1 **chicken** or **veg stock cube**, crumbled

1 teaspoon **dried basil**

1. Put the rice on to cook with the pilau rice seasoning (see p20).
2. Heat the oil in a frying pan and fry the onions and garlic until soft.
3. Add the chicken and cook until the chicken is no longer pink. Add the mushrooms and cook for 2 minutes. Season with salt and pepper.
4. Add the cream, stock cube and basil. Cook gently for 5 minutes, stirring occasionally.
5. Serve with rice.

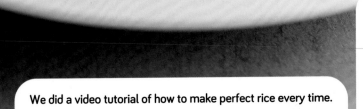

We did a video tutorial of how to make perfect rice every time.

SCAN ME

£1.65 /PERSON

EASE
★★☆☆☆

 SERVES 1

PREP 20 MINS

HAWAIIAN RISOTTO

Make the leftover pineapple into a smoothie or just eat. Tinned fruit still has lots of good stuff in it.

1/2 mug **basmati rice**

1/2 teaspoon **pilau rice seasoning** (optional)

1 tablespoon **olive oil**

1 **egg**, beaten

1 small **onion**, chopped

2–3 **mushrooms**, sliced

1/4 **red pepper**, sliced

2 **pineapple slices**, cut into pieces

1 teaspoon **soy sauce**

1 slice **cooked ham**, cut into pieces

1 **tomato**, cut into chunks

1 teaspoon **dried coriander** leaves

1 Cook the rice with the pilau rice seasoning (see p20).

2 Heat the oil in a frying pan, add the egg to it, and allow it to spread thinly over the base of the pan. It will cook in less than a minute. Once cooked, take out of the pan, cut into strips and leave to one side.

3 Add a little more oil to the pan and fry the onions until they are soft.

4 Add the mushrooms and peppers and cook for 30 seconds.

5 Add the cooked rice, pineapple, soy sauce, ham, egg, tomato and coriander leaves. Heat through gently. Season with salt and pepper.

CHORIZO RICE

If you can't find diced chorizo, you can get whole chorizo at the deli counter of most supermarkets. Just chop into bits.

£1.55 /PERSON

EASE
★★☆☆☆

SERVES
2

PREP
15 MINS

1 tablespoon **olive oil**

100g **diced chorizo**

1 **onion**, cut into wedges

2 cloves **garlic**, chopped

150g **mushrooms**, sliced

2/3 mug **basmati rice**

4 tablespoons **Philadelphia garlic and herb cream cheese**

1 **chicken stock cube**

1 1/3 mugs **water**

1 Heat the oil in a frying pan and add the chorizo, onions and garlic and fry until things begin to brown.

2 Add the mushrooms to the pan and fry for 1 minute.

3 Add the rice and fry for 1 minute. Season with salt and pepper.

4 Add the Philadelphia, stock and water and bring to the boil.

5 Turn down and simmer, with a lid on the pan, for 10 minutes.

SALMON PASTA

You can sometimes buy packs of small pieces of salmon. They are much cheaper and would be excellent for this dish.

EASE
★★☆☆☆

SERVES
1

PREP
15 MINS

2 bunches **tagliatelle pasta**

1 tablespoon **olive oil**

1 small piece **salmon**

3 **spring onions**, chopped

2 tablespoons **double cream**

1 teaspoon **dried chives**

1   Put the tagliatelle on to cook (see p21). Drain and return to the pan.

2   Heat the oil in a frying pan and fry the salmon (if you have a small piece it should only take 2–3 minutes each side). Add the spring onions to the pan towards the end of the cooking time and allow them to brown a little.

3   Remove the pan from the heat and gently break up the salmon. Add the cream and chives and return to the heat. As soon as the cream begins to bubble, add the pasta and stir everything together. Allow the pasta to heat through. This should take around 1 minute.

4   Season well with salt and pepper.

TUNA AND MUSHROOM SPAGHETTI

Don't stir the tuna too much, or it will become mushy.

- 2 portions **spaghetti** (see p21)
- 1 tablespoon **olive oil**
- 1 small **onion**, sliced
- 5–6 **mushrooms**, sliced
- 1/2 mug **frozen peas**, defrosted
- 2 teaspoons **dried chives**
- 3 tablespoons **Greek yogurt**
- 185g tin **tuna**, drained
- juice of 1/2 **lemon**
- 1/2 mug grated **Parmesan**

1 Put the spaghetti on to cook (see p21). Drain and return to the pan.

2 Meanwhile, heat the oil in a wok and fry the onion until it begins to soften. Add the mushrooms, peas and chives and cook for 1 minute. Season well.

3 Take the pan off the heat and add the yogurt, tuna, lemon juice and grated Parmesan. Stir gently. Add to the drained spaghetti. Stir gently and serve.

SCAN ME

For more of Joy's fish recipes

£ 1.10
/PERSON

EASE
★☆☆☆☆

SERVES
2

PREP
15 MINS

V OPTION

WALDORF SALAD

If you have never tried grapes in a salad, you have to try this one.

1 tablespoon **olive oil**

1 **chicken breast**, cut into chunks
or 100g **Quorn pieces**

1 **Granny Smith apple**, cored and
thinly sliced

1 **Cos lettuce**, sliced

2 sticks **celery**, sliced

DRESSING

juice of a **lemon**

2 tablespoons **olive oil**

1 teaspoon **Dijon mustard**

2 tablespoons **Greek yogurt**

salt and **pepper**

50g **pecans**, roughly chopped

100g **green grapes**, halved

1 Heat the oil in a frying pan. Add the chicken and fry until browned.

2 Mix together the apple, lettuce and celery in a bowl along with the
combined dressing ingredients. Divide between your plates.

3 Top with the chicken, walnuts and grapes.

CURRIED CHICKEN SALAD

Any leftovers can be eaten cold or used in sandwiches the next day.

£1.64 /PERSON

EASE
★☆☆☆☆

SERVES 2

PREP
15 MINS

1 tablespoon **olive oil**

1 **red onion**, chopped

1 clove **garlic**, finely chopped

2 **chicken breasts**, cut into small pieces

1 teaspoon **soy sauce**

juice of $^1/_2$ **lime**

1 teaspoon **Korma curry paste**

2 teaspoons **brown sugar**

1 teaspoon **dried coriander**

bag of **salad leaves**

1 Heat the oil in the frying pan and fry the onion and garlic until soft.

2 Add the chicken and fry until the meat is no longer pink.

3 Add the rest of the ingredients. Season with salt and pepper. Cook for 2 minutes. Serve with the salad leaves.

£2.13 /PERSON

EASE
★☆☆☆☆

SERVES 1

PREP 10 MINS

PRAWN COUSCOUS SALAD

You need to add plenty of tasty things to couscous, plus some kind of dressing or sauce.

1/2 mug **couscous**

1 mug **boiling water**

1 **tomato**, chopped

2 **spring onions**, chopped

1/4 **red** or **green pepper**, chopped

1 teaspoon **olive oil**

juice of 1/2 **lemon**

1 teaspoon **dried chives**

1/4 x 300g pack **frozen prawns**, defrosted

3cm **cucumber**, cut into cubes

salad to serve

1 Put the couscous in a bowl and add the boiling water. Cover with a plate and leave to stand for about 4 minutes. All the water should be absorbed into the couscous.

2 To make the dressing, mix the oil, lemon and chives together. Season with salt and pepper.

3 Mix all the ingredients together and serve with a green salad.

TUNA SALAD

You can add other ingredients: cucumber, tomatoes, or some fresh chilli, to spice it up a little.

£1.28 /PERSON

EASE
★☆☆☆☆

SERVES 2

PREP 15 MINS

1 mug **pasta** (we used fusilli)

1 mug **frozen peas**

4–5 **spring onions**, chopped

1 **red pepper**, chopped

3 tablespoons **mayo**

185g tin **tuna**, drained

1 teaspoon **dried chives**

1 Cook the pasta (see p21), add the peas in the same pan and simmer for a further 2 minutes. Drain and cool.

2 Flake the tuna and season with salt and pepper.

3 Mix all the ingredients together.

4 Serve with lettuce and tomatoes.

£0.38 /PERSON

EASE
★★☆☆☆

SERVES
2

PREP
15 MINS

POTATO SALAD

Serve with sausages, cold meats and green salad. Ideal with barbecue food.

2 medium **potatoes**, chopped into small cubes

3 dessertspoons **mayo**

2 tablespoons **crème fraîche**

1 teaspoon **dried chives**

1 teaspoon **dried mint**

4–5 **spring onions**, chopped

1 Put the potatoes in a pan of boiling, salted water and simmer for 10 minutes. Drain and leave to cool.

2 Mix the mayo and crème fraîche together. Add the chives and mint.

3 Add the onions and mix everything together. Season well.

SALSA SALAD

As soon as the eggs are cooked, remember to rinse them under cold water, as this stops the yolks going black around the edges.

£1.34 /PERSON

EASE
★★☆☆☆

SERVES
2

PREP
20 MINS

2 **eggs**

2 medium **potatoes**, or 8 small **new potatoes**

4 **tomatoes**

3 **spring onions**, chopped

1 teaspoon **dried chives**

juice of $1/2$ **lemon**

2 tablespoons **olive oil**

4 rashers **unsmoked bacon**

$1/2$ **curly leaf lettuce**

1 Hard-boil the eggs (see p28), peel and cut into 4 pieces.

2 Cut the potatoes into bite-size chunks, put them in boiling, salted water and then simmer for 10–15 minutes. Drain and leave to cool.

3 Make the salsa, using 2 of the tomatoes. Chop them into quite small pieces. Put in a bowl and add the chopped spring onions, chives, lemon juice and olive oil. Season with salt and pepper and mix well.

4 Fry or grill the bacon until it is crisp, then cut into bite-size pieces.

5 Cut the remaining tomatoes into chunks.

6 Wash and drain the lettuce and arrange on the two plates. Arrange the tomatoes, potatoes, bacon and eggs on the top. Pour the salsa over the top and serve.

£1.06
/PERSON

EASE
★★☆☆☆

SERVES
2

PREP
15 MINS

HOT POTATO SALAD

No need to peel or scrub the potatoes. This can be a meal in itself if served with green salad.

3 medium **potatoes**, or 6 **new potatoes**, cut into chunks

1 tablespoon **olive oil**

5 **mushrooms**, sliced

4 rashers **bacon**

5 **spring onions**, chopped

1 teaspoon **dried parsley**

DRESSING

2 tablespoons **olive oil**

1 teaspoon **wholegrain mustard**

1 tablespoon **white wine vinegar**

1. Put the potatoes in boiling, salted water, simmer for 10 minutes and drain.

2. Heat the oil in a frying pan and fry the mushrooms until they are browned. Set to one side.

3. Fry the bacon until brown and then cut into small pieces.

4. Mix the bacon, mushrooms, onions, parsley and potatoes, taking care not to break the potatoes up too much.

5. Mix the dressing ingredients together. Pour over the top.

FRUITY TUNA SALAD

Take care not to mix the tuna too vigorously as it will end up very mushy.

£2.12 /PERSON

EASE
★★☆☆☆

SERVES 2

PREP 20 MINS

2 **eggs**

DRESSING

2 tablespoons **olive oil**

juice of a **lemon**

1 teaspoon **sugar**

salt and **pepper**

SALAD

227g tin **pineapple chunks**, drained

185g tin **tuna**, drained

2 sticks **celery**, sliced

4 **spring onions**, chopped

1/2 mug **pecans**, halved

1 **Little Gem lettuce**

1 Hard boil the eggs (see p28). Peel and cut into quarters.

2 Combine the dressing ingredients.

3 Mix the salad ingredients together.

4 Serve with the dressing over the top.

SCAN ME

See our video tutorial on how to boil an egg

£ 1.67 /PERSON

EASE
★☆☆☆☆

SERVES
2-3

PREP
20 MINS

SMOKED MACKEREL PASTA SALAD

You can buy cooked, smoked mackerel in vacuum packs. Usually found with the fresh fish in the supermarket. If unopened, they will keep in the fridge for quite a while.

1½ mugs **pasta** (we used fusilli)

½ x 300g pack **green beans**, trimmed and cut in half

2 tablespoons **crème fraîche**

1 tablespoon **mayo**

1 teaspoon **dried chives**

zest and juice of ½ **lemon**

250g pack **cooked, smoked mackerel**

¼ **cucumber**, chopped

2 **spring onions**, chopped

1 Put the pasta on to boil (see p21). Add the beans 5 minutes before the end of the cooking time. Once cooked, drain, run under a cold tap and place in a bowl.

2 Mix together the crème fraîche, mayo, chives, lemon zest, juice and season with salt and pepper. Add to the pasta and mix.

3 Peel the skin off the backs of the mackerel fillets and then gently flake the fish. Add to the bowl, along with the cucumber and onions. Mix gently and serve.

LIME TUNA COUSCOUS

Don't stir tinned tuna too much as it tends to go mushy. Allow it to stay in recognizable pieces. To deseed a cucumber, cut in half lengthways and scoop out the seeds with a small spoon.

£1.58 /PERSON

EASE
★★☆☆☆

SERVES 2

PREP 20 MINS

¾ mug **couscous**

1 **veg stock cube**, dissolved in 1½ mugs of **hot water**

zest and juice of a **lime**

1 teaspoon **sugar**

2 tablespoons **olive oil**

185g tin **tuna**, drained

125g **cherry tomatoes**, halved

7cm piece **cucumber**, sliced

200g tin **sweetcorn**, drained

1 Place the couscous and lime zest in a bowl and pour over the boiling water and crumbled vegetable stock cube. Put a plate over the top to keep the heat in and leave to stand for 5 minutes.

2 Mix together the lime juice, sugar and olive oil to make a dressing. Season with salt and pepper.

3 Once the couscous is cooked, add the tuna, tomatoes, cucumber, sweetcorn and the dressing to the couscous. Stir and serve.

£ 1.05 /PERSON

EASE
★★☆☆☆

SERVES
2

PREP
15 MINS

SPAGHETTI PUTANESCA

No need to add salt to this dish as the anchovies and capers are very salty.

spaghetti (see p21)
1 tablespoon **olive oil**
1 clove **garlic**, chopped
1 small **onion**, chopped
50g tin **anchovies**, drained and sliced
1 tablespoon **capers**

$^{1}/_{2}$ **fat red chilli**, chopped
200g tin **chopped tomatoes**
10 **black olives**, halved
1 tablespoon freshly chopped **basil**
shaved **Parmesan** to serve

1. Put the spaghetti on to cook (see p21).
2. Heat the oil in a wok, or large frying pan, add the garlic and onion, and fry for 2 minutes.
3. Add the anchovies and capers and fry for 30 seconds.
4. Add the chilli, tomatoes and olives and simmer for 2 minutes. Add the basil and stir. Take off the heat.
5. Once the spaghetti is cooked, drain and add to the sauce and stir.
6. Sprinkle the Parmesan over the top.

BACON AND EGG PASTA

As soon as the hard-boiled eggs are cooked, drain and run under cold water. This stops them from going black around the yolk.

£0.83 /PERSON

EASE
★★☆☆☆

SERVES
2

PREP
25 MINS

1 mug **pasta** (we used penne)

2 **eggs**

1 tablespoon **olive oil**

4 rashers **bacon**

3 **mushrooms**, sliced

1 tablespoon **olive oil**

2 tablespoons **mayo**

3 **spring onions**, chopped

1 To cook the pasta and the eggs using the same pan, boil the water and add the eggs first and then the pasta 2 minutes later. Then cook everything together for 10 minutes.

2 Heat the oil in a frying pan and fry the bacon until crisp and remove from the pan. Add the mushrooms and fry until browned.

3 Cut the bacon into bite-size pieces.

4 Mix the oil and mayo together. Season with salt and pepper.

5 Drain the pasta and eggs and run the eggs under cold water. Take the shells off the eggs and cut each into four.

6 Mix everything together and serve.

BROKE BUT HUNGRY

Waiting for pay day, or is the loan rapidly running out? Here are some inexpensive dishes to keep the hunger pangs at bay.

SAUSAGE SOUP

When reheating sausages, make sure they are heated through well and are piping hot.

£0.78 /PERSON

EASE
★★☆☆☆

SERVES
1-2

PREP
20 MINS

1 tablespoon **olive oil**

1 small **onion**, chopped

1½ mugs **water**

1 **beef stock cube**

¼ mug **pasta**, (we used fusilli)

4 **sausages** (spicy sausages work well with this recipe)

200g tin **baked beans**

1 tablespoon **Worcestershire sauce**

1 Heat the oil in a saucepan and fry the onion.

2 Add the water, stock cube and pasta, bring to the boil and simmer gently for 4–5 minutes.

3 While the pasta is simmering, cook the sausages. Fry, or grill them, and cut into bite-size chunks.

4 Add the cooked sausages, beans and Worcestershire sauce. Cook for 2 minutes. Season with salt and pepper.

SCAN ME

For more soup recipes

£0.80 /PERSON

EASE
★☆☆☆☆

SERVES
1

PREP
25 MINS

HAM AND VEG SOUP

The ingredients listed make a good combination, but you can use whatever vegetables you have to hand.

25g **butter**, measure using packet

½ medium **onion**, chopped

1 small **potato**, cut into cubes

1 stick **celery**, cut into pieces

1 medium-sized **carrot**, peeled and sliced

1 dessertspoon **flour**

1½ mugs **water**

½ **veg** or **chicken stock cube**

¼ mug **frozen peas**

1 slice **ham**, chopped

1 Heat the butter in a saucepan and fry the onion for 1 minute.

2 Add the potatoes, celery and carrots and cook for about 1 minute.

3 Add the flour and mix in with the vegetables already in the pan.

4 Add the water and stock cube, season well and bring to the boil. Simmer for 10 minutes, or until the vegetables are cooked.

5 Add the peas and cook for 2 minutes.

6 Add the pieces of ham and cook for 1 minute (omit if vegetarian).

7 Serve with bread.

ITALIAN SOUP

£0.49 /PERSON

EASE ★☆☆☆☆

SERVES 2-3

PREP 25 MINS

V

The ingredients for this soup may seem a little complicated. Don't worry if you don't have them all. The celery and the spinach can be left out if you wish.

25g **butter**, measure using packet

1 **onion**, chopped

1 **potato**, diced

1 **carrot**, diced

1/2 **red pepper**, chopped

1–2 sticks **celery**, sliced

2 cloves **garlic**, finely chopped

400g tin **chopped tomatoes**

1 tablespoon **tomato purée**

3 mugs **water**

1 **veg stock cube**, crumbled

1 portion **spaghetti** (see p21), broken into pieces

1 teaspoon **dried basil**

2 pieces defrosted **frozen spinach**

1 Melt the butter in a saucepan, add the onions, potato, carrot, pepper, celery and garlic and cook for two minutes, stirring well. Season with salt and pepper.

2 Add the chopped tomatoes, tomato purée, water and stock cube and bring to the boil. Simmer for 10 minutes, then add the uncooked spaghetti and herbs and simmer for a further 6 minutes.

3 Add the spinach, bring back to the boil, and season well with salt and pepper.

£1.32 /PERSON

EASE
★★★★☆

SERVES
2-3

PREP
20 MINS

COOK
30 MINS

V OPTION

LAMB COBBLER

If you like the topping, it can be used, instead of potatoes, with other recipes such as Shepherd's Pie or Monday Pie.

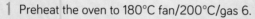

1 tablespoon **olive oil**

1 **onion**, chopped

250g **lamb** or **Quorn mince**

400g tin **chopped tomatoes**

1 teaspoon **mixed dried herbs**

1 tablespoon **tomato purée**

1 mug **self-raising flour**

1/2 mug **suet**

pinch **salt**

1 teaspoon **dried basil** or **coriander**

1/2 mug **water**

1 **egg**, beaten or **milk**

1 Preheat the oven to 180°C fan/200°C/gas 6.

2 Heat the oil in the frying pan and fry the onion until soft.

3 Add the mince and cook until the meat is no longer pink. Season with salt and pepper.

4 Add the chopped tomatoes, herbs, tomato purée and season with salt and pepper. Simmer for 5 minutes and transfer to a casserole dish.

5 To make the dumplings, put the flour, suet, salt and herbs in a bowl and stir well. Add the water slowly, until it makes a soft ball.

6 Turn out onto a floured surface, and form into six balls.

7 Place them on the top of the meat mixture and brush the top with beaten egg or milk to help it brown. If you do not have a pastry brush, use your fingers!

8 Bake for 25–30 minutes, or until browned.

PASTA WITH SPICY SAUSAGES

You can use vegetarian sausages with this recipe and add ½ teaspoon chilli powder at step 4.

EASE
★★☆☆☆

SERVES
2

PREP
20 MINS

V OPTION

1 mug **pasta** (we used penne)

1 tablespoon **olive oil**

6 **spicy pork**, **beef** or **vegetarian sausages**

1 small **onion**, sliced

1 clove **garlic**, chopped

400g tin **chopped tomatoes**

1 tablespoon **tomato purée**

1 teaspoon **mixed herbs**

1 Put the pasta on to cook (see p21). Drain and return to the pan.

2 Heat the oil in a pan and fry the sausages. Then take them out of the pan and cut them into bite-size pieces.

3 Fry the onions and garlic for 1–2 minutes. Season with salt and pepper.

4 Add the chopped tomatoes, tomato purée and herbs to the pan and bring to the boil. Allow to simmer for 4–5 minutes for the flavours to blend.

5 Add the sausages and pasta to the pan and cook for a further 2–3 minutes until everything is heated through.

£0.80 /PERSON

EASE
★★★☆☆

SERVES 2

PREP 20 MINS

V

CHEESE AND ONION ROSTI

You can make Rosti with just potatoes, potatoes and onion, or potatoes and cheese.

2 large **potatoes**, grated

1 **onion**, grated

1/2 mug grated **Cheddar cheese**

1 **egg**, beaten

1 teaspoon **dried basil**

1 tablespoon **olive oil**

bag of **salad leaves**

2 **spring onions**, sliced

3 **tomatoes**, sliced or 8 **cherry tomatoes**, halved

1 Squeeze the excess water from the potatoes and onion and mix with the cheese, egg and basil. Season with salt and pepper.

2 Divide into four and form into 'cakes'.

3 Heat the oil in the frying pan and cook on a medium heat for 5 minutes each side.

4 Serve with salad.

CHICKPEA AND CHORIZO COUSCOUS

Couscous is so easy to cook, but you need to add plenty of flavour to it.

£0.91 /PERSON

EASE
★★☆☆☆

SERVES
2-3

PREP
15 MINS

1/2 mug **couscous**

1 **veg stock cube**, dissolved in a mug of **boiling water**

1/2 teaspoon **paprika**

1/2 teaspoon **cumin**

1/2 teaspoon **ground coriander**

1/2 tablespoon **olive oil**

1 small **onion**, sliced

1 clove **garlic**, finely chopped

2 **chorizo sausages**, chopped

400g tin **chickpeas**, rinsed and drained

2 **tomatoes**, roughly chopped

1/4 mug **water**

1 Put the couscous in a bowl and add the boiling water, stock cube, paprika, cumin and coriander. Stir together. Cover with a plate and leave to stand for at least 5 minutes, until the water is absorbed.

2 Heat the oil in a frying pan or wok. Add the onions, garlic and chopped chorizo. Fry until the chorizo is browned.

3 Add the chickpeas, tomatoes and water and cook for another 1–2 minutes, stirring frequently. Most of the liquid should be gone.

4 Add the couscous, mix together and serve.

£0.96 /PERSON

EASE
★★★☆☆

SERVES
2

PREP
15 MINS

COOK
25 MINS

V OPTION

SAUSAGE PIE

There is no need to peel the potatoes for this recipe. The skins add a little extra flavour.

2 large **potatoes**, diced

25g **butter**, measure using packet

1 tablespoon **olive oil**

4 **pork** or **vegetarian sausages**

1 small **onion**, chopped

2 cloves **garlic**, finely chopped

1 **leek**, sliced

1 **veg stock cube**

1/2 mug **hot water**

1 teaspoon **cornflour**

1/2 mug grated **Cheddar cheese**

1 Put the potatoes in a saucepan of boiling, salted water and simmer for 10 minutes, drain and return to the pan. Add the butter and shake the potatoes in the pan to distribute it. Leave to one side.

2 Preheat the oven to 180°C fan/200°C/gas 6.

3 Heat the oil in a frying pan and fry the sausages until browned. Remove from pan and cut into bite-size pieces.

4 Using the same frying pan, fry the onion and garlic for 2–3 minutes. Add the leek and cook for a further 2–3 minutes.

5 Add the vegetable stock cube and hot water and bring to the boil.

6 Mix the cornflour with a couple of tablespoons of cold water and then add to the frying pan, stirring well. The sauce should thicken slightly. Season well with salt and pepper.

7 Put the sausages back into the pan and stir. Pour into a casserole dish. Pile the potatoes on the top and sprinkle over with grated cheese. Bake for 25–30 minutes until the cheese has browned.

SCAN ME

Pies rock! Joy has some more pie recipes

£1.09
/PERSON

EASE
★★☆☆☆

SERVES
1

PREP
20 MINS

V
OPTION

SPICY RISOTTO

If you like hot food, you can add more curry paste.

1 mug **water**

¹/₂ mug **basmati rice**

¹/₂ teaspoon **pilau rice seasoning** (optional)

1 tablespoon **olive oil**

1 small **onion**, chopped

1 clove **garlic**, finely chopped

125g **beef**, **lamb** or **Quorn mince**

¹/₂ **beef**, **lamb** or **veg stock cube**

1 dessertspoon **mild curry paste**

2 **mushrooms**, sliced

¹/₄ mug **water**

1 Cook the rice with pilau rice seasoning (see p20).

2 Heat the oil in a frying pan and fry the onion and garlic for 1 minute.

3 Add the mince and cook until it is no longer pink.

4 Add the stock, curry paste, mushrooms and the ¹/₄ mug of water. Bring to the boil and simmer gently for 3–4 minutes until all the liquid has gone. Stir frequently.

5 Add the cooked rice and mix. Season well with salt and pepper.

SPAGHETTI BOLOGNESE

£1.01 /PERSON

EASE ★★☆☆☆

SERVES 2

PREP 20 MINS

V OPTION

'Spag Bol' is a must to master. If you cook enough sauce for two, you can either share it with a flatmate, or the next day, add either curry paste or chilli and eat with rice or baked potatoes.

1 tablespoon **olive oil**

1 **onion**, chopped

2 cloves **garlic**, chopped

250g **beef** or **Quorn mince**

400g tin **chopped tomatoes**

1 tablespoon **tomato purée**

5 **mushrooms**, sliced

1 **beef** or **veg stock cube** , crumbled

1 teaspoon **dried mixed herbs**

spaghetti (see p21)

1 Heat the oil in a frying pan and fry the onion and garlic for 1 minute.

2 Add the mince and cook until the meat is no longer pink.

3 Add the rest of the ingredients, apart from the spaghetti, season with salt and pepper, and stir. Simmer gently for 10 minutes.

4 Put the spaghetti on to cook (see p21).

5 Serve.

£1.24 /PERSON

EASE
★★☆☆☆

SERVES 2

PREP 25 MINS

TUNA HASH

A good way to make one tin of tuna go a long way. Won't reheat too well, so make and share.

2 medium **potatoes**, cut into cubes

25g **butter**, measure using packet

1 tablespoon **olive oil**

1/2 **red onion**, sliced

185g tin **tuna**, drained

200g tin **sweetcorn**, drained

1 Put the potatoes in a pan of boiling, salted water and simmer for 8–10 minutes until they are tender. Drain and return to the pan. Add the butter and gently stir around.

2 Heat the oil in a frying pan and fry the onions until they begin to brown. Season with salt and pepper.

3 Add the potatoes, sweetcorn and tuna to the pan and gently stir.

4 Heat on a medium heat and allow the hash to brown and then stir in the brown bits. Repeat twice. Don't keep stirring the hash, or the tuna will go mushy.

BIG WRAPS

£1.79 /PERSON

EASE
★★★☆☆

SERVES
2-3

PREP
20 MINS

V OPTION

¹/₂ mug **basmati rice**

1 tablespoon **olive oil**

1 **onion**, finely chopped

4 **mushrooms**, sliced

1 **red** or **yellow pepper**, chopped

1 **chicken breast**, cut into small pieces, or
Quorn pieces

200g tin **sweetcorn**, drained

4 **tortilla wraps**

¹/₂ mug grated **Cheddar cheese**

avocado salsa (see p155)

1 Put the rice on to cook (see p20).

2 Heat the oil in a frying pan and fry the onions for 2–3 minutes until they begin to soften. Add the mushrooms and pepper and continue to cook for 2–3 minutes.

3 Add the chicken, or Quorn, and cook until it is no longer pink.

4 Add the rice and the drained sweetcorn and cook for 2–3 minutes. Season with salt and pepper.

5 Warm the tortilla wraps in a microwave for 20 seconds.

6 Serve everything on the tortillas with salsa on top.

£1.28 /PERSON

SAUSAGE AND EGG BAKE

Eggs don't microwave too well. They tend to go a bit rubbery, so best to share this one.

EASE
★★☆☆☆

SERVES 2

PREP 15 MINS

COOK 20 MINS

V OPTION

6 **herby**, **spicy** or **vegetarian sausages**

1 **onion**, chopped

1 clove **garlic**, finely chopped

400g tin **chopped tomatoes**

1 teaspoon **tomato purée**

400g tin **cannellini beans**, rinsed and drained

1 teaspoon **dried basil**

2 **eggs**

1 Preheat the oven to 180°C fan/200°C/gas 6. Grease a casserole dish.

2 Fry the sausages in a frying pan until browned. Remove from pan.

3 Fry the onion and garlic for 2–3 minutes, stirring frequently.

4 Add the chopped tomatoes, tomato purée and beans, stir and bring to the boil. Simmer for 2–3 minutes.

5 Cut each sausage into 4 and add to the pan, stir well and take off the heat. Add the basil and season well with salt and pepper.

6 Pour the mixture into the casserole dish. Break the 2 eggs over the top of the mixture.

7 Bake in the oven for 15–20 minutes until the eggs are cooked.

8 Serve with fresh, crusty bread or baked potatoes.

SCAN ME

For more bake recipes and ideas

CORN FRITTERS WITH CHILLI SAUCE

The dipping sauce is so easy and you can use it with other things; tortilla chips or patties, for example.

DIPPING SAUCE

2 teaspoons **cornflour**

1/2 mug **water**

1 **fat red chilli**, deseeded and chopped

1 **spring onion**, finely chopped

2 tablespoons **white wine vinegar**

2 tablespoons **tomato purée**

2 tablespoons **sugar**

4 tablespoons **flour**

2 **eggs**

200g tin **sweetcorn**, drained

2 **spring onions**, chopped

1 small **courgette**, diced quite small

1/2 x 200g block **feta cheese**, crumbled

1 tablespoon **olive oil**

green salad and **dressing** to serve

1 To make the dipping sauce, mix the cornflour with the water in a small saucepan. Add the rest of the sauce ingredients and bring to the boil, stirring frequently. Turn down the heat and simmer for 1–2 minutes. Leave to cool.

2 To make the fritters, beat together the flour and eggs; it should be quite thick. Add the drained sweetcorn, spring onions, courgette and crumbled feta cheese. Season with salt and pepper.

3 Heat the oil in a frying pan. Make the fritters by adding the mixture, about 1 tablespoon at a time, to the hot oil. Spread them out a little and fry on medium heat for 1–2 minutes each side. The fritters should be nicely browned and cooked through.

4 Serve with the chilli sauce.

SCAN ME

Joy has more vegetarian recipes

ONE-POT DISHES

Tired of washing up loads of pots and pans? These 'one-pot' dishes will minimise the clearing-up process.

SAUSAGE AND BACON CASSEROLE

Reheats well the next day, you can eat this with rice.

£1.57 /PERSON

EASE
★★☆☆☆

SERVES 2-3

PREP 30 MINS

---

1 tablespoon **olive oil**

6 **sausages**

6 slices **streaky bacon**

1 **onion**, sliced

1 clove **garlic**, finely chopped

1 **courgette**, cut into bite-size chunks

400g tin **chopped tomatoes**

1 tablespoon **tomato purée**

1 **fat red chilli**, thinly sliced

1 **chicken stock cube**

1/2 mug **water**

400g tin **butter beans**, rinsed and drained

crusty bread

---

1 Heat the oil in a wok, or large frying pan, and fry the sausages and bacon until both are browned. Remove from the pan and cut each sausage into 3. Cut the bacon into small pieces.

2 Tip off any excess oil from the pan and fry the onions and garlic for 2–3 minutes.

3 Add the courgettes, tomatoes, tomato purée and chilli to the pan and cook for 3–4 minutes. Season with salt and pepper.

4 Return the sausages and bacon to the pan, add the stock, water and butter beans. Bring to the boil, season with pepper (the bacon will be salty enough). Turn down to simmer for 10 minutes.

5 Serve together with crusty bread.

£1.06
/PERSON

EASE
★★☆☆☆

SERVES
2

PREP
20 MINS

V OPTION

SIMPLE CHILLI CON CARNE

Serve with rice, jacket potatoes or crusty bread. I guess, not technically a 'one-pot', but you get the idea…

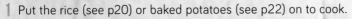

rice to serve (see p20) or
2 large **potatoes**

1 tablespoon **olive oil**

1 large **onion**, chopped

2 cloves **garlic**, finely chopped

250g **beef** or **Quorn mince**

400g tin **chopped tomatoes**

1 **beef**, **lamb** or **veg stock cube**

2 teaspoons **chilli powder**, less, if you like it not so hot

400g tin **baked beans**

1 Put the rice (see p20) or baked potatoes (see p22) on to cook.

2 Heat the oil in a frying pan and fry the onion and garlic for 1 minute.

3 Add the mince and cook until the meat is no longer pink. Season with salt and pepper.

4 Add the chopped tomatoes, stock cube and chilli powder. Cook for 10 minutes.

5 Add the beans and cook for a further one minute. Taste to see if you would like more chilli powder. If you add more, cook for another few minutes.

6 Serve with rice or baked potatoes.

CHICKEN HOT POT

You can add other flavourings to the stock; for example, 2 teaspoons curry paste, or a teaspoon of chilli powder.

 £1.31 /PERSON

 EASE ★☆☆☆☆

 PREP 10 MINS

4 **chicken thighs**

3 **carrots**, sliced

3 medium **potatoes**, cut into chunks

2 sticks **celery**, chopped

1 **onion**, cut into 6 wedges

2 cloves **garlic**, left whole

1 tablespoon **Worcestershire sauce**

1 **chicken stock cube**, dissolved in a mug of **hot water**

SERVES 2

PREP 10 MINS

COOK 75 MINS

1 Preheat the oven to 190°C fan/220°C/gas 7.

2 Put all the ingredients in a casserole dish. Season with salt and pepper.

3 Cover with a lid, or foil, and cook for 45 minutes.

4 Take the lid off and cook for a final 30 minutes to let things brown.

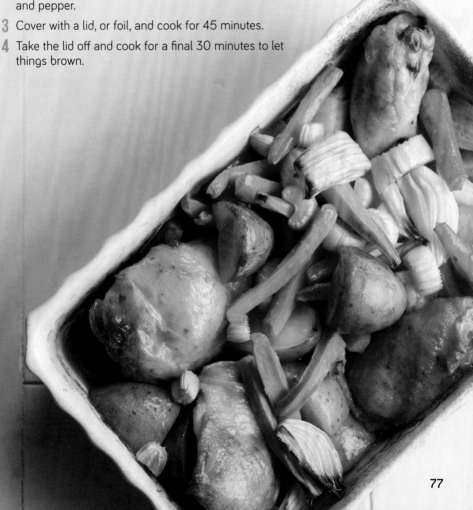

£1.44 /PERSON

EASE
★★☆☆☆

SERVES 2

PREP
30 MINS

PANCETTA AND BROAD BEAN RISOTTO

Don't use margarine instead of the butter. The rice absorbs the flavour of the butter, whereas margarine has little taste.

25g **butter**, measure using packet

1 **onion**, chopped

1 clove **garlic**, finely chopped

250g **pancetta lardons**

1 mug **risotto rice**

2 **tomatoes**, chopped

2 mugs **hot water**

1 **veg stock cube**

1 mug **frozen broad beans**

1/2 mug grated **Parmesan cheese**

1 Melt the butter in a frying pan and fry the onions and garlic until they become soft.

2 Add the pancetta lardons and fry for one minute.

3 Add the rice, cook until the butter is absorbed into the rice.

4 Add the tomatoes, stock and water and season with pepper. The pancetta lardons will give enough saltiness.

5 Simmer for 10–12 minutes, stirring every now and then. You may need to add more liquid. Risottos should be creamy, not dry.

6 Add the broad beans and bring back to simmer for 5 minutes.

7 Take off the heat and stir in the grated Parmesan.

TUNA AND LEMON PASTA

£1.56 /PERSON

EASE
★☆☆☆☆

SERVES 2

PREP 25 MINS

Cooking the beans and the pasta in the same pan saves a bit of washing up. All together, a one-pot dish.

1 mug **pasta** (we used farfalle)

½ x 200g pack **green beans**

1 mug **frozen peas**

185g tin **tuna**, drained

zest and juice of a **lemon**

2 **spring onions**, chopped

1 teaspoon **dried chives**

½ x 300g pot **crème fraîche**

a little **Parmesan**

1 Put the pasta on to cook (see p21). Add the green beans 5 minutes before the end of the cooking time and the peas 3 minutes before the end. Drain and return to the pan.

2 Drain the oil from the tin of tuna. Add to the pan, along with the lemon juice and zest, spring onions, chives, crème fraîche and salt and pepper. Gently mix together, so as not to break up the tuna too much.

3 Serve with a little grated Parmesan over the top.

SCAN ME

Joy has done more fish recipes

£0.89
/PERSON

EASE
★★☆☆☆

SERVES
2

PREP
15 MINS

COOK
15 MINS

V OPTION

SAUSAGE WITH APPLE AND MUSTARD

This is a very simple, inexpensive 'all in one-pot' meal to make.

1 tablespoon **olive oil**

4–6 **pork**, **herby** or **vegetarian sausages**

1 small **onion**, sliced

2 medium **potatoes**, cut into chunks

1 **eating apple**, cut into chunks

1 teaspoon **wholegrain mustard**

2 tablespoons **sweet chutney**, e.g. Branston pickle

1 **veg stock cube**, dissolved in a mug of **hot water**

1 Heat the oil in a wok, or frying pan, and fry the sausages until browned on all sides. Take them from the pan and cut into chunks.

2 Tip out any excess oil and fry the onions and potatoes until they begin to brown.

3 Add the apples, mustard, chutney, stock and water and return the sausages to the wok. Bring everything to the boil and then turn down the heat and simmer for 10–15 minutes, until the potatoes are cooked. Stir a couple of times during the cooking process. Season well with salt and pepper and serve.

BOSTON BEANS

Great as a simple snack and a DIY twist on traditional 'beans on toast'.

EASE
★★☆☆☆

SERVES
2

PREP
15 MINS

1 tablespoon **olive oil**

100g **smoked, streaky bacon**

1 small **onion**, sliced

1 clove **garlic**, chopped

400g tin **black-eyed beans**, rinsed and drained

1 tablespoon **brown sugar**

1 tablespoon **white wine vinegar**

1 teaspoon **Dijon mustard**

400g tin **chopped tomatoes**

bread rolls or **toast** to serve

1 Heat the oil in a large frying pan and fry the bacon until it is browned. Remove from the pan and cut into small pieces.

2 Add the onion and garlic and fry until the onions begin to soften.

3 Add the rest of the ingredients, season with salt and pepper, bring to the boil and then turn down to simmer for 5 minutes.

4 Serve on toast, or with bread rolls.

£1.23 /PERSON

EASE
★★★☆☆

SERVES
4

PREP
30 MINS

SPINACH AND FETA FRITTATA

Frittatas are very versatile, as you can add lots of different things. They are also a good way of making a meal in only one pan.

100g **lardons** or **chopped streaky bacon**

1 tablespoon **olive oil**

340g tin **sweetcorn**, drained

200g **frozen spinach**, about 16 small pieces, defrosted and well drained

8 **eggs**

200g pack **feta**, crumbled

1/2 x 250g pack **cherry tomatoes**, halved

DRESSING

juice of a **lime**

2 tablespoons **olive oil**

1 teaspoon **sugar**

salt and **pepper**

green leaf salad to serve

1 Heat the oil in a frying pan and fry the lardons until they begin to brown.

2 Add the sweetcorn and spinach to the pan and cook for 1 minute. Season with salt and pepper.

3 Preheat the grill.

4 Beat the eggs, pour into the pan and cook. As the egg begins to set, gently move so the unset egg reaches the bottom of the pan.

5 While some of the egg is still runny, add the feta and tomatoes. Do not stir after this point.

6 Place the pan under the grill and cook until the egg is set and the top begins to brown. This should take 5–10 minutes.

7 Cut into wedges and serve with the combined salad dressing ingredients and the salad.

SCAN ME

Never made frittata before? Here's
another one you might like to try

£0.97 /PERSON

EASE
★★☆☆☆

SERVES 2

PREP 25 MINS

V OPTION

CHICKEN KORMA COUSCOUS

If you have leftovers, they are best eaten cold the next day and not reheated.

1/2 mug **couscous**

1 **chicken** or **veg stock cube**, dissolved in a mug of **boiling water**

2 tablespoons **olive oil**

1 small **onion**, chopped

1/2 **red pepper**, chopped

1 **chicken breast**, cut into chunks or 100g **Quorn pieces**

1 1/2 tablespoons **Korma curry paste**

1 tablespoon **water**

1/3 mug **ready-to-eat dried apricots**, chopped

1 Cover the couscous with the boiling water and crumbled stock cube in a bowl and cover with a plate. Leave to stand for at least 5 minutes until the water is absorbed.

2 Heat the oil in a frying pan or wok. Add the onions and peppers and cook until the onions begin to soften. Season with salt and pepper.

3 Add the chicken breast and cook until no longer pink.

4 Add the Korma paste, water and apricots and cook for 30 seconds, stirring frequently.

5 Stir in the couscous, season well and serve.

MEDITERRANEAN CHICKEN TRAYBAKE

Sometimes the skins on chicken thighs can produce a lot of fat. If so, just scoop off with a spoon before serving.

£ 1.41 /PERSON

EASE
★☆☆☆☆

SERVES 2

PREP 15 MINS

COOK 50 MINS

4 **chicken thighs**

1 **onion**, cut into wedges

3 large **potatoes**, cut into chunks

1 clove **garlic**, finely chopped

3 **tomatoes**, quartered

12 **olives**, chopped

1 teaspoon **dried basil**

2 tablespoons **olive oil**

1 **chicken stock cube**, dissolved in 1/2 mug of **boiling water**

paprika to sprinkle over

1 Preheat the oven to 180°C fan/200°C/gas 6.

2 Put all the ingredients, except the stock and paprika, in a casserole dish. Season with salt and pepper. Distribute the oil evenly and arrange the pieces so that the skins of the chicken will brown. Add the stock and sprinkle the casserole with paprika.

3 Put in the oven for 45–50 minutes until the chicken is browned and cooked through. Test one piece to make sure.

TASTE OF HOME

Missing home and never thought you would? Here are a few ideas to remind you of something nice and familiar.

ROAST POTATOES AND SAUSAGES

You can just use this recipe to make great roast potatoes.

£0.85 /PERSON

EASE ★☆☆☆☆

SERVES 2

PREP 10 MINS

COOK 50 MINS

V OPTION

1 tablespoon **olive oil**

3 medium **potatoes**, cut into chunks

6 **beef**, **pork** or **vegetarian sausages**

1 **onion**, cut into wedges

400g tin **baked beans**

1 Preheat the oven to 180°C fan/200°C/gas 6.

2 Oil the casserole dish, or baking tray, and place the potatoes, sausages and onions in it. Distribute the oil over everything, using your hands. Season well with salt and pepper.

3 Put in the oven for 30 minutes. Take out of the oven and carefully turn things over, so that they brown on the other side. Cook for a further 20 minutes, or until everything is browned.

4 Serve with baked beans.

£1.73 /PERSON

EASE
★★☆☆☆

SERVES 2-3

PREP 5 MINS

COOK 105 MINS

V OPTION

ROAST CHICKEN

This recipe is for two to three people. If you just cook for yourself, use less vegetables and the leftover chicken can be used the next day in sandwiches.

1.5kg **whole chicken**,

4 large **potatoes**, cut into chunks

2 **red onions**, cut into wedges

2 tablespoons **olive oil**

1 teaspoon **dried rosemary** (optional)

1 Preheat the oven to 180°C fan/200°C/gas 6.

2 Place the chicken in an oiled, flat, roasting dish or casserole dish. Add the potatoes and onion and brush with oil. Season with salt and pepper and the rosemary. Cover with foil.

3 Cook for 45 minutes.

4 Remove the foil and cook for a further 30–45 minutes, to allow everything to brown.

5 Serve with green vegetables if you want.

SPICY SLOPPY JOES

Classic comfort food with a bit of an Indian twist.

£0.62 /PERSON

EASE
★★☆☆☆

SERVES 2

PREP 20 MINS

V OPTION

1 tablespoon **olive oil**

1 small **onion**, peeled and sliced

1 clove **garlic**, finely chopped

250g **beef** or **Quorn mince**

½ teaspoon **cumin**

½ teaspoon **coriander**

½ teaspoon **cinnamon**

½ **fat red chilli**, chopped

2 teaspoons **plain flour**

1 **beef** or **veg stock cube**

½ mug **water**

naan breads

Greek yogurt

1 Heat the oil in a frying pan and add the onions and garlic. Fry until the onions begin to soften.

2 Add the mince and cook until it is no longer pink, stirring frequently.

3 Add the cumin, coriander, cinnamon and chilli. Season with salt and pepper and cook for 1 minute.

4 Add the flour and mix well, then add the stock cube and water and bring to the boil. Turn down and simmer for 5 minutes. Stir every now and then.

5 Meanwhile, sprinkle a little water on the naan bread and grill for 1 minute each side.

6 Serve with the naan and some yogurt.

£0.88 /PERSON

EASE
★★★☆☆

SERVES
2

PREP
10 MINS

COOK
50 MINS

V OPTION

MONDAY PIE

If you are a vegetarian, leave out the Worcestershire sauce.

1 tablespoon **olive oil**

1 **onion**, sliced

250g **beef** or **Quorn mince**

1 **beef** or **veg stock cube**,

400g tin **baked beans**

1 tablespoon **Worcestershire sauce**

3–4 medium **potatoes**, thinly sliced

1 Preheat the oven to 180°C fan/200°C/gas 6.

2 Heat the oil in a frying pan and fry the onion for 1 minute.

3 Add the mince, or Quorn, and cook until the mince is no longer pink, or the Quorn heated through. Season with salt and pepper.

4 Add crumbled stock cube, but no water. Stir well. The cube will dissolve in the meat mixture.

5 Add the tin of beans and Worcestershire sauce and pour into a casserole dish.

6 Layer the potatoes on top of the meat and cook for 50 minutes. Test the potatoes with a fork to check that they are cooked. If not, turn the oven down to 160°C fan/180°C/gas 4 and cook for another 10 minutes.

LANCASHIRE HOT POT

Bit of a lengthy cooking time, so plan ahead. Well worth the wait.

£1.87 /PERSON

EASE
★★☆☆☆

SERVES 2

PREP 10 MINS

COOK 90 MINS

1 tablespoon **olive oil**

1 **onion**, cut into 6 wedges

2 cloves **garlic**, finely chopped

250g **cubed stewing lamb**, or **lamb mince**

1 tablespoon **flour**

2 mugs **water**

1 **veg stock cube**

2 **carrots**, peeled and cut into chunks

3 medium **potatoes**, cut into chunks

1 Preheat the oven to 180°C fan/200°C/gas 6.

2 Heat the oil in a frying pan and fry the onions and garlic until they brown slightly. Add the meat and cook until the outside is no longer pink.

3 Add the flour and stir well.

4 Add the water and the stock cube. Bring to the boil. The liquid should thicken.

5 Add the carrots and potatoes to the mixture. Season with salt and pepper.

6 Transfer to a casserole dish with a lid and cook for 1½ hours. If you use lamb mince, you will only need to cook for 1 hour.

£1.13 /PERSON

EASE
★☆☆☆☆

SERVES
2-3

PREP
10 MINS

COOK
20 MINS

V OPTION

MULLIGATAWNY SOUP

If you reheat this soup the next day, make sure that it boils and then simmers slowly for about 3–4 minutes. Alternatively, reheat in a microwave for 2 minutes on a high setting.

1 tablespoon **olive oil**

1 small **onion**, chopped

1 **carrot**, peeled and sliced

1 stick **celery**, cut into small pieces

1 eating **apple**, cut into chunks

1 tablespoon **curry paste** (mild)

1/2 teaspoon **ground coriander**

3 mugs **water**

1 **chicken** or **veg stock cube**

400g tin **chopped tomatoes**

1/4 mug **basmati rice**

1 **chicken breast**, cut into small pieces, or 100g **Quorn pieces**

1 Heat the oil in a frying pan and fry the onion, carrot and celery until they begin to soften. Season with salt and pepper.

2 Add the rest of the ingredients and bring to the boil. Simmer for 20 minutes, stirring occasionally.

CHEESY POTATOES

Cook the potatoes in a fairly large dish so that there is more surface area to brown on the top.

£0.89 /PERSON

EASE
★★☆☆☆

SERVES
1-2

PREP
10 MINS

COOK
35 MINS

V

---

3 medium **potatoes**, thinly sliced
1 x **Quick Cheese Sauce** (see p28)

½ mug grated **Cheddar cheese**
bacon or **sausages** (optional)

---

1 Preheat the oven to 180°C fan/200°C/gas 6.

2 Arrange the sliced potatoes in layers in the bottom of the casserole dish.

3 Pour the cheese sauce over and season with salt and pepper.

4 Top with grated cheese.

5 Bake in the oven for 35–40 minutes, or until the potatoes are cooked and the cheese is browned. Test the potatoes with a fork. If they are not cooked, leave in the oven for another 10 minutes.

6 Non-vegetarians can serve with fried bacon or sausages.

£2.50
/PERSON

QUICK SHEPHERD'S PIE

This is an easy way to make Shepherd's Pie without the fuss of mashed potatoes.

EASE
★★☆☆☆

SERVES
2

PREP
20 MINS

COOK
25 MINS

V OPTION

500g **lamb**, **beef**, or **Quorn mince**

1 mug **water**

1 tablespoon **gravy granules**

6 medium **potatoes**, cut into chunks

25g **butter**, measure using packet

1 mug grated **Cheddar cheese**

1 Preheat the oven to 180°C fan/200°C/gas 6.

2 Put the mince into a pan with the water and bring to the boil. Simmer for 10–15 minutes. Add the gravy granules and stir. Season with salt and pepper.

3 Put the potatoes in a separate pan, with enough water to cover them. Boil for 10 minutes and then drain. Add the butter and mix.

4 Pour the mince into the bottom of a casserole dish.

5 Carefully spoon the potatoes onto the top and sprinkle with the cheese.

6 Cook for 20–25 minutes until the top is browned.

CHICKEN CASSEROLE

Quick and easy to prepare. Leave it in the oven whilst you relax.

£1.28 /PERSON

EASE
★★☆☆☆

SERVES 2
PREP 10 MINS
COOK 60 MINS

1 tablespoon **olive oil**

4 **chicken thighs**

1 **onion**, sliced

400g tin **chopped tomatoes**

2 cloves **garlic**, finely chopped

4–5 **mushrooms**, sliced

1 dessertspoon **Worcestershire sauce**

1 teaspoon **mixed dried herbs**

baked potatoes or **rice** to serve (see p22 or p20)

1. Preheat the oven to 180°C fan/200°C/gas 6.

2. Heat the oil in a frying pan and fry the chicken until brown on both sides. Transfer into a casserole dish.

3. Fry the onions until soft. Add the chopped tomatoes, garlic, mushrooms, Worcestershire sauce and herbs. Season with salt and pepper.

4. Bring to the boil and then transfer to the casserole. Put a lid on and bake for 1 hour. If you are having baked potatoes, put those in the oven now.

5. Serve with rice, or baked potatoes, and green vegetables.

TOAD IN THE HOLE WITH ONION GRAVY

The secret of good Toad in the Hole is a hot oven and hot fat!

EASE
★★★★☆

SERVES
2-3

PREP
20 MINS

COOK
35 MINS

V OPTION

BATTER

1½ mugs **plain flour**

3 **eggs**, beaten

1 dessertspoon **wholegrain mustard** (optional)

pinch of **salt**

½ mug **milk**

2 x 2cm cubes **white Flora** or 2 tablespoons **olive oil**

6 **pork** or **vegetarian sausages**

1 tablespoon **olive oil**

1 **red** and 1 **white onion**, sliced

1 dessertspoon **flour**

1 **beef** or **veg stock cube**

1 mug **water**

1 Preheat the oven to 220°C fan/240°C/gas 9.

2 Beat together the batter ingredients in a large bowl. Add water a little at a time, mixing between additions, until the batter is the consistency of single cream.

3 Put the oil, or white Flora, in a casserole dish. Place the sausages evenly apart in the dish. Place the dish in the oven for 5–7 minutes. The fat should be smoking a little after this time.

4 Gently add the batter to the casserole dish. It should bubble around the edges.

5 Return the dish to the oven and cook for 25 minutes, or until nicely browned. The mixture should rise around the edges.

6 While the toad is cooking, make the onion gravy. Heat the oil in a saucepan and add the onions. Fry for 5–6 minutes until they have softened and become quite brown. Season well with salt and pepper.

7 Add the flour and stir well. Add the stock cube and water. Bring to the boil. The gravy should thicken.

SCAN ME

We've done a video tutorial on how to
make a different gravy. Check it out

£1.98 /PERSON

FISHERMAN'S PIE

Fish goes a bit rubbery when reheated, so this one is best shared.

EASE
★★★☆☆

SERVES 2

PREP
20 MINS

COOK
20 MINS

2 **eggs**

4 medium **potatoes**, diced

25g **butter**, measure using packet

1 mug **milk**

2 pieces **cod** or **haddock fillet** (defrost if frozen)

2 teaspoons **cornflour**

1 teaspoon **dried parsley** or **basil**

1 mug grated **Cheddar cheese**

1 Preheat the oven to 200°C fan/240°C/gas 7.

2 Cook the eggs and potatoes in the same pan: boil the eggs for two minutes and then add the diced potatoes and cook for a further for 8–10 minutes. Drain and take out the eggs. Then add the butter to the potatoes and stir gently.

3 Run the eggs under cold water and peel and quarter them.

4 Place the milk and fish in a frying pan and simmer gently for approximately 5 minutes, or until the fish turns from opaque to white.

5 Mix the cornflour with 2 tablespoons of cold milk and add to the pan. Stir. The sauce will thicken. Gently break up the fish and season with salt and pepper.

6 Add the hard-boiled eggs and herbs. Mix together and pour into a casserole dish.

7 Place the potatoes on the top of the fish mixture and top with the grated cheese.

8 Cook for 20 minutes. The top should be browned.

9 Serve with green vegetables.

£2.21 /PERSON

EASE
★★★☆☆

SERVES
2

PREP
20 MINS

CAJUN CHICKEN GUMBO

Gumbos are often time consuming dishes to make, but we have switched to using chicken breasts here which speeds up the cooking time dramatically.

1 mug **basmati rice**

2 **chicken breasts**, cut into bite-size pieces

2 teaspoons **Cajun seasoning**

2 tablespoons **olive oil**

1 **onion**, sliced

1 **green pepper**, chopped

1 clove **garlic**, finely chopped

50g **diced chorizo**

400g tin **chopped tomatoes**

2 teaspoons **dried mixed herbs**

1 Put the rice on to cook (see p20).

2 Mix the chicken and Cajun seasoning.

3 Heat the oil in a frying pan and fry the onion, pepper and garlic until they begin to brown.

4 Add the chicken and chorizo and fry for 3–4 minutes until the chicken is cooked through.

5 Add the tomatoes and herbs, season with salt and pepper, and simmer for 3 minutes.

6 Serve with the rice.

TUNA AND PASTA BAKE

You can use different condensed soups; celery or chicken, for example.

£1.35 /PERSON

EASE
★☆☆☆☆

SERVES
2-3

PREP
15 MINS

COOK
20 MINS

2 mugs **pasta** (we used fusilli)

185g tin **tuna**, drained

295g tin **condensed cream of mushroom soup**

2 packets **ready-salted crisps**

½ mug grated **Cheddar cheese**

1 Preheat the oven to 200°C fan/220°C/gas 7.

2 Put the pasta on to cook (see p21).

3 Drain and place back in the saucepan. Add the tuna and condensed soup (do not dilute the soup). Mix together and season with salt and pepper.

4 Transfer to a casserole dish.

5 Crush the crisps in the bag, mix with the grated cheese, and sprinkle on top of the mixture in the casserole dish.

6 Cook in the oven for 20 minutes until the cheese and crisps are browned.

£1.79 /PERSON

CHICKEN PARCELS WITH MINI ROASTS

If you add other vegetables to this recipe, and they usually take a long time to cook, remember to cut them small.

SERVES 2

PREP 10 MINS

COOK 25 MINS

4 medium **potatoes**, cut into cubes	4 **sun-dried tomatoes**, chopped
1 tablespoon **olive oil**	4 spring **onions**, chopped
2 **chicken breasts**	juice of **lemon**
10 **olives**	1 tablespoon **olive oil**
8 **cherry tomatoes**	1 teaspoon **dried basil**

1 Preheat the oven to 200°C fan/220°C/gas 7.

2 Place the potatoes on a baking tray. Sprinkle with salt and pepper, drizzle over the oil and then mix with your hands to distribute evenly. Place in the oven for 25–30 minutes or until browned.

3 Take a large, doubled sheet of aluminium foil. Place the chicken breast in the middle. Add the olives, cherry tomatoes, sun-dried tomatoes and onions. Squeeze the lemon juice over the chicken mixture, drizzle over the oil and sprinkle over the basil. Season well with salt and pepper.

4 Seal up the foil parcel by pinching it together. Place the parcel on a baking tray and cook in the oven for 25 minutes. Carefully open the parcel, it will be full of very hot steam. Check that the chicken is cooked in the centre. If not cooked, return to the oven for a few more minutes and check again.

5 Serve with the potatoes, using the juices from the parcel as a sauce.

SCAN ME

So you have cooked all the chicken recipes in this book and need more of Joy's simple, delicious recipes.

SPICY SOUP AND DUMPLINGS

EASE ★★★★☆

SERVES 2-3

PREP 30 MINS

V

You can use this dumpling recipe with other soups, or in stews. Don't stir the soup too much, or you will break up the dumplings.

1 tablespoon **olive oil**

1 large **onion**, chopped

1 large **potato**, cut into chunks

1 large **carrot**, peeled and sliced

400g tin **chopped tomatoes**

1 **veg stock cube**, crumbled

2 teaspoons **curry paste**

2 mugs **water**

3–4 **mushrooms**, sliced

DUMPLINGS

1 mug **self-raising flour**

1/2 mug **suet**

salt and **pepper**

1 teaspoon **dried coriander** or **basil**

1 **egg** + **water** to mix up to 1/2 mug

1 Heat the oil in a large saucepan and fry the onions. Add potatoes and carrots and cook until the onions begin to soften.

2 Add the chopped tomatoes, stock cube, curry paste, water and mushrooms. Season with salt and pepper. Bring to the boil and leave to simmer gently while you make the dumplings.

3 In a large bowl, mix the flour, suet, salt, pepper and coriander.

4 In a mug, beat the egg and the water.

5 Add just enough of the egg and water to the bowl to form a soft ball of dough when mixed. Don't make it too wet.

6 Put some extra flour onto your work surface and turn the mixture out onto it. Form into a large ball, cut into 8 pieces, forming each one into dumplings.

7 Add these to the simmering soup and cook gently, with a lid on the pan, for 10–15 minutes.

SCAN ME

Joy did a video tutorial on how to make dumplings.

£1.57 /PERSON

EASE
★★★☆☆

SERVES
2

PREP
15 MINS

COOK
90 MINS

BEEF STEW

Cooking the baking potatoes at the same time as the stew makes the meal simple and saves a bit of electricity/gas.

1 tablespoon **olive oil**

1 **onion**, sliced

1 **carrot**, peeled and sliced

350g **cubed stewing steak**

1 tablespoon **flour**

1 **beef stock cube**, dissolved in a mug of **hot water**

400g tin **chopped tomatoes**

2 large **potatoes**

1 Preheat the oven to 180°C fan/200°C/gas 6.

2 Heat the oil in a pan and fry the onions and carrots until they begin to brown. Add the meat and cook until it is no longer pink.

3 Sprinkle the flour over the ingredients in the pan. Stir for one minute, making sure that the flour is evenly distributed.

4 Add the water and stock cube. Stir well, then add the chopped tomatoes. The sauce should thicken a little, but will thicken more as it cooks in the oven. Season with salt and pepper.

5 Place in a casserole dish, cover with a lid and place in the oven for 45 minutes.

6 After 45 minutes, put the potatoes in the oven and cook everything for a further hour.

SAUSAGES AND CHEDDAR MASH WITH ONION GRAVY

You need to peel potatoes to get good mash. Mash does not need to be too smooth. If you mash the potatoes too much, they will become glutinous and sticky. The onion gravy can be used with other recipes.

£1.01 /PERSON

EASE
★★☆☆☆

SERVES
2

PREP
35 MINS

V OPTION

6 **pork** or **vegetarian sausages**

4 medium **potatoes**, peeled and cut into chunks

1/2 mug grated **Cheddar cheese**

25g **butter**, measure using packet

1 dessertspoon **olive oil**

25g **butter**, measure using packet

1 **onion**, sliced

1 teaspoon **flour**

1 mug **water**

1/2 **beef** or **veg stock cube**, crumbled

1 Preheat the oven to 200°C fan/220°C/gas 7. Lightly grease a baking tray and place the sausages on it. Season with salt and pepper. Bake in the oven for 30 minutes.

2 Put the potatoes into boiling, salted water and simmer for 10–15 minutes until tender. Drain and return them to the pan. Add the butter and cheese. Mash with a potato masher, or a large fork. Put the lid back on the pan and keep warm until the sausages are cooked.

3 While the potatoes are cooking, make the onion gravy. Heat the oil and butter in a saucepan, add the onion and fry until it is quite brown. You will need to stir frequently. Add the flour and stir until evenly distributed. Add the water and stock cube. Stir well and bring to the boil, the gravy should thicken slightly. Season well.

£1.98
/PERSON

EASE
★★★☆☆

SERVES
2

PREP
15 MINS

COOK
90 MINS

BACON AND EGG BAKE

This is best shared on the day you cook it, as the eggs do not microwave well.

1 mug **pasta** (we used cavatappi)

1 head **broccoli**, cut into florets

1/2 x 250g pack **cherry tomatoes** halved, or 2 large **tomatoes**, chopped

1/2 mug **milk**

1/2 x 300g **Philadelphia cream cheese**

1 mug grated **Cheddar cheese**

1 teaspoon **mixed herbs**

8 rashers **streaky bacon**

2 or 3 **eggs**

1 Preheat the oven to 200°C fan/220°C/gas 7. Grease a casserole dish.

2 Put the pasta on to cook (see p21). Add the broccoli after 5 minutes. Cook for a further 5 minutes, drain and return to the pan. Add the tomatoes.

3 Mix together the milk, cream cheese and half the grated Cheddar cheese. Heat very gently to melt the cream cheese. Add the herbs, season well with salt and pepper, and pour into the pasta and broccoli.

4 Fry the bacon until it is crisp. Cut into bite-size pieces and add to the pasta mix. Mix gently and pour into the casserole dish.

5 Make hollows in the pasta mix and break the eggs into them. Sprinkle the rest of the Cheddar cheese over the top.

6 Put in the oven and bake for 20 minutes.

CHILLI TORTILLA PIE

Good 'movie-watching' food. Be careful not to overcook the cheese topping, as the cheese still needs to be soft and stretchy.

£1.48 /PERSON

EASE ★★☆☆☆

SERVES 2

PREP 35 MINS

V OPTION

---

2 tablespoons **olive oil**

2 **carrots**, peeled and chopped

1 **onion**, sliced

1 clove **garlic**, finely chopped

500g **beef** or **Quorn mince**

400g tin **chopped tomatoes**

1 tablespoon **tomato purée**

1 **beef** or **veg stock cube**, crumbled

½ mug **water**

½ teaspoon **chilli powder**

½ x 225g bag **tortilla chips**

1 mug grated **Cheddar cheese**

---

1 Heat the oil in a wok or saucepan. Fry the carrots, onion and garlic until the onion begins to soften.

2 Add the minced beef and cook until no longer pink.

3 Add the tomatoes, tomato purée, stock cube, water and chilli powder. Season with salt and pepper and simmer gently for 15 minutes.

4 Preheat the oven to 200°C fan/220°C/gas 7.

5 Pour the chilli mixture into a casserole dish. Place the tortilla chips on top and then sprinkle the cheese on top.

6 Place in the oven for 5 minutes until the cheese has melted.

VEGETARIAN

Searching for some interesting meat-free dishes?
Treat your veggie friends to something special.

CHICKPEA CURRY WITH MINT RAITA

£1.08 /PERSON

EASE ★★☆☆☆

SERVES 2-3

PREP 25 MINS

V

Using fresh mint in the raita is always going to be best, but it is OK to use dried if that is all you have.

---

1 tablespoon freshly chopped **mint** or
1 teaspoon **dried mint**

4 tablespoons **natural yogurt**

1 mug **basmati rice**

1 tablespoon **olive oil**

1 **onion**, chopped

1 **potato**, cubed

2 cloves **garlic**, finely chopped

1 **eating apple**, cored and cut into chunks

400g tin **chickpeas**, rinsed and drained

1 mug **water**

2 tablespoons **curry paste**

1 **veg stock cube**, crumbled

1 **courgette**, sliced

1/4 mug **sultanas**

4 **mushrooms**, sliced

1 tablespoon **tomato purée**

---

1 Make the raita by mixing the mint and yogurt.

2 Put the rice on to cook (see p20).

3 Heat the oil in a wok, or frying pan, and fry the onion until soft.

4 Add the potatoes, garlic, apple and chickpeas. Cook in the oil for 2–3 minutes. Season with salt and pepper.

5 Add the water, curry paste and stock cube, bring to the boil and then simmer for 10 minutes.

6 Add the courgette, sultanas, mushrooms and tomato purée. You may need to add a little more water. Cook for 5 minutes.

vegetarian **111**

VEGETABLE BAKE

You can use any mixture of vegetables for this dish. Make sure that there are some that you can fry at the beginning, as this gives more taste. Boil vegetables which take longer to cook, eg. carrots, potatoes, parsnips, etc.

£1.57 /PERSON

EASE
★★☆☆☆

SERVES 2-3

PREP 15 MINS

COOK 25 MINS

V

1 **carrot**, sliced	4 **mushrooms**, sliced
1 **sweet potato**, cut into chunks	1/2 **red** or **green pepper**, sliced
1 head **broccoli**, broken into florets	1 **courgette**, sliced
1/2 mug **frozen peas**	2 teaspoons **HP sauce**
1 tablespoon **olive oil**	2 x **Quick Cheese Sauce** (see p31)
1 **onion**, chopped	1/2 mug grated **Cheddar cheese**

1 Preheat the oven to 180°C fan/200°C/gas 6.

2 Put the carrots and sweet potato into a pan of boiling, salted water. Simmer for 5 minutes and add the broccoli and peas. Simmer for another 5 minutes. Drain well.

3 Heat the oil in a frying pan and fry the onions until soft. Add the mushrooms, peppers and courgette. Cook for 2 minutes.

4 Mix all the vegetables together and place in a casserole dish. Sprinkle with HP sauce and season well.

5 Make the Quick Cheese Sauce and pour over the vegetables.

6 Sprinkle the grated cheese over the top and bake in the oven for 20–25 minutes. The cheese should be browned on top.

BREAKFAST BURRITOS

This makes four burritos, so can serve two, or four people, depending on how hungry you are.

£2.63 /PERSON

EASE
★★★☆☆

SERVES 2

PREP 20 MINS

V

tomato and onion salsa - buy or make (see p155)

1 tablespoon **olive oil**

1 small **red onion**, sliced

1 **red pepper**, sliced

400g tin **black-eyed beans**, rinsed and drained

25g **butter**, measure using packet

6 **eggs**

4 **soft tortillas**

4 tablespoons **soured cream**

1 **avocado**, peeled and sliced

½ mug grated **Cheddar cheese**

1 If you are going to make your own salsa, make it now (see p155).

2 To make the filling, heat the oil in a frying pan and fry the onion and pepper for 2 minutes. Add the beans, heat through, and set aside.

3 Scramble the eggs in a saucepan (see p28).

4 Arrange everything on the tortillas.

£0.85 /PERSON

EASE
★★☆☆☆

SERVES 2

PREP
15 MINS

COOK
20 MINS

V

CRISP TOPPED PASTA AND CHEESE BAKE

If you are not a vegetarian, you could add a teaspoon of Worcestershire sauce to the cheese sauce.

1 x **Quick Cheese Sauce** (see p31)

1 mug **pasta** (we used fusilli)

1 **egg**, beaten

1 teaspoon **dried chives**

½ teaspoon **mustard**

2 **tomatoes**, each cut into 8

1 packet **plain crisps**

½ mug grated **Cheddar cheese**

1 Preheat the oven to 180°C fan/200°C/gas 6.

2 Make the Quick Cheese Sauce and leave to cool a little.

3 Put the pasta on to cook (see p21).

4 Add the beaten egg, chives and mustard to the cheese sauce.

5 Put the drained pasta and tomatoes into a casserole dish, or ovenproof bowl. Pour the sauce over the top.

6 Crush the crisps in the bag and mix with the grated cheese. Sprinkle on the top of the pasta.

7 Cook in the oven for 20 minutes. The cheese and the crisps should be browned.

SIMPLE VEG AND PASTA SALAD

Good for barbecues, or with cold meats, sausages and other salads.

£0.27 /PERSON

EASE ★☆☆☆☆

SERVES 4

PREP 15 MINS

V

1 mug **pasta** (we used fusilli)

1/2 **red onion**, finely chopped

3 tablespoons **mayo**

1 **red pepper**, chopped

2 teaspoons **dried basil** or **chives**

2 sticks **celery**, finely sliced

1 Put the pasta on to cook (see p21). Drain and rinse under cold water.

2 Prepare the other ingredients and mix them all together with the pasta.

3 Season well.

RICE AND APPLE SALAD

This is an ideal accompaniment to barbecues, or can be eaten with cold meats, sausages, baked potatoes, potato wedges or green salads.

SERVES 4

PREP 15 MINS

V

1 mug **basmati rice**

1 teaspoon **pilau rice seasoning** (optional)

2 tablespoons **olive oil**

juice of ½ **lemon**

1 teaspoon **dried chives**

3–4 **spring onions**, chopped

2 tablespoons **raisins**

200g tin **sweetcorn**, drained

2 **eating apples**, cut into small chunks

1 Cook the rice with the pilau rice seasoning (see p20).

2 Leave the rice to cool.

3 Mix the oil, lemon juice and chives together. Season with salt and pepper.

4 Mix all the ingredients together. Serve.

PINE NUT PASTA BAKE

Good one to make for your vegetarian friends when they come over.

£2.73 /PERSON

EASE
★★☆☆☆

SERVES 2

PREP 15 MINS

COOK 25 MINS

1½ mugs **pasta** (we used fusilli)

25g **butter**, measure using packet

1 tablespoon **flour**

1 mug **milk**

150g **garlic and herb Philadelphia cheese**

½ teaspoon **paprika**

1 teaspoon **mixed herbs**

1 tablespoon **olive oil**

1 medium **onion**, sliced

100g pack **pine nuts**

1 mug grated **Cheddar cheese**

1 Preheat the oven to 180°C fan/200°C/gas 6. Grease a casserole dish.

2 Put the pasta on to cook (see p21).

3 Heat the butter in a saucepan and add the flour. Stir well and cook for 30 seconds. Take off the heat, add the milk and stir well. Gently bring to the boil, stirring frequently.

4 Add the Philadelphia, paprika and herbs to the sauce and mix until smooth. Season with salt and pepper.

5 Heat the oil in a frying pan and fry the onions and pine nuts until they begin to brown. Add to the cheese sauce.

6 Drain the pasta and stir in the cheese sauce mix. Pour into a casserole dish and sprinkle the Cheddar cheese over the top.

7 Place in the oven for 20–25 minutes until the cheese is browned on the top.

V

£0.85 /PERSON

EASE
★★★☆☆

SERVES 2

PREP
15 MINS

COOK
15 MINS

V

CAULIFLOWER AND BROCCOLI CHEESE

You can eat this on its own, but you could also eat it with some nice, crusty bread to mop up all of the cheese sauce at the end.

1 head **cauliflower**, broken into florets
1 head **broccoli**, broken into florets

2 x **Quick Cheese Sauce** (see p31)
1/2 mug grated **Cheddar cheese**

1 Preheat the oven to 200°C fan/220°C/gas 7.

2 Put the cauliflower and broccoli in a saucepan of boiling, salted water and simmer for 5–7 minutes (see p18).

3 Make the Quick Cheese Sauce (see p31).

4 Put the drained vegetables in a greased casserole dish and pour the sauce over them. Top with grated cheese and put in the oven for 10–15 minutes until browned on top.

CLASSIC NUT ROAST

You can use a variety of nuts in this recipe, but cashews, Macadamians or Brazil nuts seem to work the best, as they have a slightly sweeter taste than other nuts.

£1.52 /PERSON

EASE
★★★☆☆

SERVES 2

PREP 10 MINS

COOK 20 MINS

V

1 tablespoon **olive oil**

1 small **onion**, finely chopped

2 **mushrooms**, finely chopped

2 slices **wholemeal bread**

200g pack **cashew nuts**, chopped

1 teaspoon **Marmite**

1 teaspoon **dried mixed herbs**

1/2 **veg stock cube**, dissolved in 1/2 mug **boiling water**

1 Preheat the oven to 180°C fan/200°C/gas 6. Grease a small ovenproof dish.

2 Heat the oil in a frying pan and fry the onions until they begin to brown. Add the mushrooms and cook for a further 2–3 minutes. Take off the heat and season with salt and pepper.

3 Make the bread into breadcrumbs. Just chop it up finely; it does not matter if the breadcrumbs are a bit chunky. Add to the pan along with the nuts.

4 Mix the Marmite, herbs, water and stock together in a mug, until the stock and Marmite dissolve. Add to the pan and mix everything together.

5 Pour into the dish and cook in the oven for 20 minutes. The nuts should be brown on top.

£1.61 /PERSON

SPICY VEGETABLE PASTA BAKE

EASE
★★☆☆☆

SERVES 2

PREP
15 MINS

COOK
20 MINS

V

The vegetables can be varied. If you use things like potatoes and carrots, you will need to boil them before adding to the mixture.

1¹/₂ mugs **pasta** (we used conchiglie)

1 tablespoon **olive oil**

1 **onion**, chopped

2 cloves **garlic**, finely chopped

6 **mushrooms**, sliced

2 **courgettes**, sliced

¹/₂ **red** or **green pepper**, sliced

1 teaspoon **mixed herbs**

1 **red chilli**, finely chopped

1 tin **Campbell's condensed cream of tomato soup**, undiluted

¹/₂ mug grated **Cheddar cheese**

1 Preheat the oven to 200°C fan/220°C/gas 7.

2 Put the pasta on to cook (see p21).

3 Heat the oil in a frying pan and fry the onions and garlic until soft.

4 Add the mushrooms, courgettes, peppers, herbs and chilli. Cook for 2 minutes.

5 Add the tomato soup and bring to the boil. Then take off the heat and season well.

6 Drain the pasta and stir into the vegetable mixture.

7 Turn into a greased casserole dish and top with the grated cheese.

8 Cook for 25 minutes, or until the cheese is browned.

SCAN ME

For more vegetarian recipes, why not check out
Joy's other book "Vegetarian Nosh for Students"

SOMETHING FOR THE WEEKEND

Got a little more time on your hands and fancy something a bit different to eat? Treat yourself to something from this section.

MINCE HOT POT

The potatoes need to be sliced thinly, or they will not cook in the allocated time.

£1.01 /PERSON

EASE
★★★☆☆

SERVES
2

PREP
15 MINS

COOK
50 MINS

V OPTION

1 tablespoon **olive oil**

1 **onion**, chopped

250g **beef** or **Quorn mince**

400g tin **chopped tomatoes**

3–4 **mushrooms**, sliced

1 tablespoon **tomato purée**

1 teaspoon **dried basil**

1 **beef** or **veg stock cube**

4–5 medium **potatoes**, thinly sliced

1 Preheat the oven to 180°C fan/200°C/gas 6.

2 Heat the oil in a frying pan, or wok, and fry the onion for 1 minute.

3 Add the mince and cook until no longer pink. Season with salt and pepper.

4 Add the tomatoes, mushrooms, tomato purée, basil and stock cube. Bring to the boil and then transfer into a casserole dish.

5 Arrange the sliced, uncooked potatoes in layers on the top. Brush the top with oil; fingers will work if you don't have a pastry brush.

6 Cook for 45–50 minutes, the potatoes should be browned on top. Check that the potatoes are cooked. If not, turn down oven to 160°C fan/180°C/gas 4 and cook for a further 10–15 minutes.

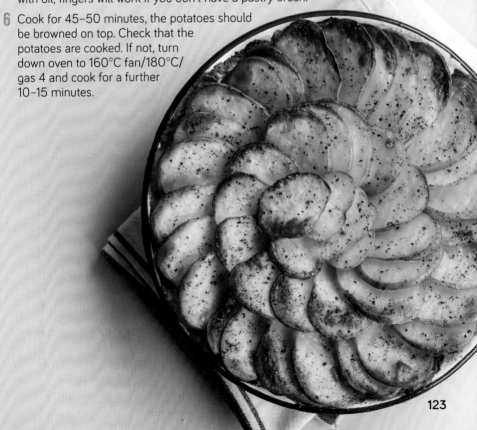

£2.35 /PERSON

SPICY COCONUT CHICKEN

A good meal to make and share. Will reheat well the next day, or freeze.

EASE
★★★☆☆

SERVES 2-3

PREP
15 MINS

COOK
40 MINS

1 tablespoon **olive oil**

6 **chicken thighs**

1 **onion**, thinly sliced

1 clove **garlic**, finely chopped

1 **fat green chilli**, deseeded and finely chopped

3 **tomatoes**, roughly chopped

1 teaspoon **turmeric**

1 teaspoon **ground cumin**

1 teaspoon **ground coriander**

juice of a **lime**

1 **chicken stock cube**

400ml tin **coconut milk**

1 mug **basmati rice**

1 Preheat the oven to 180°C fan/200°C/gas 6.

2 Heat the oil in a pan. Add the chicken and cook for about 5 minutes, until the skin begins to brown. Remove from the pan and place in a casserole dish.

3 Add the onions, garlic and chillies to the pan and fry for 3–4 minutes until the onion is soft.

4 Add the tomatoes and spices to the pan and cook for 3–4 minutes. Season with salt and pepper.

5 Add the lime juice, stock and coconut milk to the pan and bring to the boil. Season with salt and pepper. Once boiling, pour over the chicken in the casserole dish.

6 Put the casserole in the oven for 35–40 minutes.

7 15 minutes before the end of the cooking time, put the rice on to cook (see p20).

8 Take the casserole out of the oven, check for taste and season as needed. Serve with the rice.

SCAN ME

For more chicken recipes

£0.87 /PERSON

BOBOTIE

EASE
★★★☆☆

SERVES
2

PREP
15 MINS

COOK
40 MINS

V OPTION

This is great cold the next day. Best not to microwave, as it has eggs in it.

2 large **potatoes**

1 tablespoon **olive oil**

1 small **onion**, chopped

1 clove **garlic**, finely chopped

250g **beef** or **Quorn mince**

2 teaspoons **curry paste**

½ an **eating apple**, unpeeled and cut into chunks

⅓ mug **raisins**

1 dessertspoon **chutney**, Branston pickle or similar

1 **egg**, beaten + **milk** to make 1 mug

1 Preheat the oven to 180°C fan/200°C/gas 6.

2 Put the potatoes in the oven to bake (see p22).

3 Heat the oil in a frying pan and fry the onions and garlic for 1–2 minutes. Season with salt and pepper.

4 Add the mince and cook until the meat is no longer pink.

5 Add the curry paste, apple, raisins, chutney and some salt and pepper. Cook for 2 minutes. Pour into a greased casserole dish.

6 Pour the egg and milk mixture over everything in the casserole dish.

7 Cook in the oven for 40 minutes until nicely browned.

CHEDDAR AND MUSTARD BAKED CHICKEN

You must use chicken breast, as legs and thighs will not cook in the time.

2 large **potatoes**

¹/₂ mug grated **Cheddar cheese**

1 tablespoon **flour**

1 teaspoon **dried chives**

2 tablespoons **milk**

1 teaspoon **mustard**

2 **chicken breasts**

1. Preheat the oven to 200°C fan/220°C/gas 7.

2. Put the potatoes on to bake (see p22).

3. Mix together the grated cheese, flour and chives. Add the milk and mustard and mix again. Season with salt and pepper.

4. Pile the cheese mix on top of the chicken breasts. Place on a greased baking tray, or the bottom of a casserole dish. Leave until the potatoes have 30 minutes left to cook.

5. Bake in the oven, with the potatoes, for 25–30 minutes. The cheese should be browned.

6. Serve with salad.

127

PASTA AND CHICKEN BAKE

Take care not to over-bake this, as the chicken will go dry.

£2.12 /PERSON

EASE
★★☆☆☆

SERVES
2

PREP
15 MINS

COOK
30 MINS

V OPTION

1 mug **pasta** (we used penne)

1 tablespoon **olive oil**

1 **red onion**, finely chopped

4 **mushrooms**, sliced

250g packet **Philadelphia herbs and garlic cream cheese**

2 **chicken breasts**, cut into large slices or 200g **Quorn pieces**

1/4 mug **raisins**

juice of 1/2 **lemon**

1/2 mug grated **Cheddar cheese**

1 Preheat the oven to 180°C fan/200°C/gas 6.

2 Put the pasta on to cook (see p21). Drain well and return to the pan.

3 Heat the oil in a frying pan and fry the onions and mushrooms. Cook for 3-4 minutes until the onions are softened. Add to the pasta.

4 Break up the soft cheese with a fork and add to the pasta. The warmth of the pan will cause the cheese to melt slightly.

5 Add the uncooked chicken, raisins and lemon juice, season with salt and pepper, mix together and pour into a casserole dish. Sprinkle the grated cheese over the top. Bake in the oven for 25-30 minutes until golden brown.

SPICY CHICKEN MEATBALLS

£1.36 /PERSON

EASE ★★★★★

SERVES 2-3

PREP 25 MINS

This dish is a little more difficult, so try it after you have gained a bit of experience in cooking. You need to use fresh chillies, as dried ones will not taste the same.

SWEET AND SOUR SAUCE

1 mug **water**

2 tablespoons **tomato purée**

3 tablespoons **sugar**

2 tablespoons **white wine vinegar**

1 tablespoon **soy sauce**

2 teaspoons **cornflour**

1 mug **basmati rice**

2 **chicken breasts**, finely chopped

2 **spring onions**, finely chopped

1 **fat red chilli**, finely chopped

198g tin **sweetcorn**, drained

1 teaspoon **flour**

1/2 beaten **egg**

1 tablespoon **olive oil**

1 To make the sauce, put all ingredients into a saucepan and stir well to mix in the cornflour. Bring to the boil, stirring frequently. Take off the heat and leave to one side. Season with salt and pepper.

2 Put the rice on to cook (see p20).

3 To make the meatballs, mix together the chopped chicken, spring onions, chilli, sweetcorn, flour and egg, in a dish or bowl and season with salt and pepper.

4 Heat the oil in the frying pan and fry dessertspoons of the mixture on a medium heat for 5–10 minutes, turning regularly.

5 Check to see if they are cooked by cutting through one of the meatballs. If the meat is no longer pink, then they are ready.

6 Reheat the sauce and serve with the rice.

SWEET POTATO AND BACON BAKE

Exceptionally rich, sweet and moreish, in equal measure.

£1.65 /PERSON

EASE
★★★☆☆

SERVES
2

PREP
20 MINS

COOK
25 MINS

3 **sweet potatoes**, cut into chunks

50g **butter**, measure using packet

3 **eggs**

1/2 mug **milk**

100g **smoked streaky bacon**

50g **butter**, measure using packet

1 teaspoon **brown sugar**

handful of **pecans**, chopped

1 Preheat the oven to 180°C fan/200°C/gas 6.

2 Add the potatoes to a pan of boiling, salted water and simmer for 9 minutes.

3 Drain, return to the pan and add the butter. 'Squish' a bit. Turn into a greased, casserole dish.

4 Beat the eggs and milk together and add to the casserole dish.

5 Arrange the bacon on top.

6 Melt the butter and add the pecans and sugar. Mix until the sugar disolves and then sprinkle over the top of the dish.

7 Bake in the oven for 25 minutes, or until the bacon is browned.

BACON AND MUSHROOM PASTA BAKE

You can use up any spare rashers of bacon in Bacon and Egg Pasta (p55), or in Bacon and Banana sandwich (p24).

£0.99 /PERSON

EASE
★☆☆☆☆

SERVES
2-3

PREP
15 MINS

COOK
25 MINS

1 mug **pasta** (we used farfalle)

1 tablespoon **olive oil**

1 small **onion**, chopped

6 slices **streaky bacon**, cut into pieces

6–8 **mushrooms**, sliced

1/2 mug (150ml) **double cream**

3/4 mug grated **Cheddar cheese**

1 Preheat the oven to 180°C fan/200°C/gas 6.

2 Put the pasta on to cook (see p21). Drain and return to the pan.

3 While the pasta is cooking, heat the oil in a wok and fry the onions until they become soft. Add the bacon and cook until it begins to turn brown. Add the mushrooms and cook for 1 minute.

4 Take off the heat and stir in the drained pasta and the cream. Season with pepper, the bacon will provide enough salt.

5 Pour into a casserole dish and sprinkle with grated cheese. Place in the oven for 20 minutes, or until the cheese is browned.

£1.95 /PERSON

EASE
★★★☆☆

SERVES
2

PREP
20 MINS

COOK
20 MINS

COD PASTA BAKE

You can sometimes buy packs of fish pieces, either fresh or frozen, at a good price in the supermarkets. They are excellent for this recipe.

1 mug **pasta** (we used fusilli)

1 head **broccoli**, broken into 'small trees'

2–3 **cod fillets** (fresh or frozen)

1 mug **milk**

2 teaspoons **cornflour**

2 **spring onions**, chopped

1 mug **frozen peas**

1 teaspoon **dried parsley**

1/2 mug grated **Cheddar cheese**

1 Preheat the oven to 180°C fan/200°C/gas 6.

2 Cook the pasta and broccoli in the same pan for approximately 5 minutes, depending on the pasta you use (see p21).

3 Place the (defrosted) fish and the milk in a frying pan and cook gently for 3–4 minutes. Remove the fish.

4 Mix the cornflower with a tablespoon of cold milk and add to the hot milk in the pan. It should thicken.

5 Break up the fish gently and add to the thickened milk.

6 Drain the pasta and broccoli. Add to the fish mixture. Add the chopped spring onions, peas and parsley. Season with salt and pepper and stir gently.

7 Pour into a casserole dish and top with the grated cheese. Cook for 20 minutes or until the cheese is browned.

OVEN BAKED RISOTTO

You can replace the bacon lardons with pancetta lardons if you wish.

£1.74 /PERSON

EASE
★★★☆☆

SERVES 2-3

PREP 20 MINS

COOK 20 MINS

1 tablespoon **olive oil**

1 **onion**, chopped

250g **bacon lardons**

1 mug **basmati rice**

4 pieces **frozen spinach**, defrosted

2 mugs **water** + 1 **chicken stock cube**

1 teaspoon **dried basil**

3 **tomatoes**, chopped

1/2 mug grated **Parmesan cheese**

1 Preheat the oven to 200°C fan/220°C/gas 7.

2 Grease a 20x20cm casserole dish, or individual dishes.

3 Heat the oil in a frying pan and add the onions and bacon lardons. Fry until the bacon begins to brown.

4 Add the rice and allow it to absorb the oil in the pan. Season well with pepper, the bacon will give enough saltiness.

5 Squeeze the moisture out of the spinach and add to the pan with the water, stock cube, basil and tomatoes. Bring to the boil.

6 Pour into the casserole dish and cover with a lid or foil. Place in the oven for 20 minutes, or until the rice is tender.

7 Take out of the oven and stir in the Parmesan cheese.

EASE
★★★★☆

SERVES
2-3

PREP
10 MINS

COOK
90 MINS

BEER CAN ROAST CHICKEN

If there is any juice left in the roasting tray at the end, don't be tempted to try and make it into gravy. Ben tried and it didn't work!

2 tablespoons **olive oil**

1.5kg **chicken**

1 teaspoon **smoked paprika**

1 teaspoon **dried rosemary**

440ml can **lager**

4 large **potatoes**

COLESLAW

3 **carrots**, thinly sliced or grated

1 **apple**, thinly sliced or grated

1 **Romaine lettuce**, thinly sliced

4 **spring onions**, sliced

2 tablespoons **natural yogurt**

juice of a **lemon**

2 tablespoons **honey**

1 Preheat the oven to 185°C fan/205°C/gas mark 6.

2 Rub the oil over the chicken and rub in the paprika and rosemary. Season with salt and pepper.

3 Pour out half of the can of lager (you can drink it if you like!). Place the can upright on the roasting tray. Remove the string from the chicken and place over the can to make the chicken 'stand up'. Roast in the oven for 1½ hours.

4 Cut the potatoes into wedges and arrange on another roasting tray. Add 1 tablespoon of oil, season and put in the oven 30 minutes before the end of the cooking time for the chicken. Cook for 45 minutes.

5 Make the coleslaw by mixing all the ingredients together. Season well with salt and pepper.

6 Allow the chicken to rest and cool a little before removing the can from the inside.

7 Serve with the wedges and coleslaw.

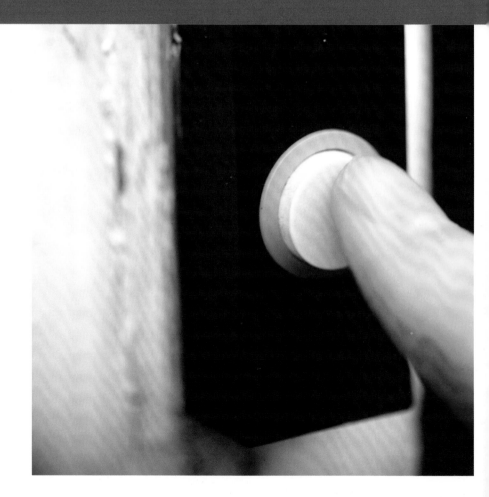

FRIENDS AROUND

Want to impress your friends, but not sure how? Here is something for when there is a hungry crowd to feed.

PANCAKES

Pancakes are easy to make and are good fun when you have friends around. Just make sure you are not the only one standing cooking them! Tossing them is always fun. Catching them not guaranteed!

£0.22 /PERSON

EASE
★★★☆☆

SERVES
2

PREP
20 MINS

V

---

2 **eggs**

6 tablespoons **self-raising flour**

milk

Trex or **white Flora** to fry (you can use oil, but a lard type is best)

---

1. Beat the eggs and flour together in a bowl or jug. Gradually add the milk, making sure there are no lumps. The mixture should be as thin as single cream, i.e. quite thin, but not as thin as milk.

2. Heat about 2cm cube of white Flora in a frying pan. When the fat begins to smoke a little, pour approximately 2 tablespoons of the mixture into the pan. Tip the pan around so that the mixture spreads over the surface of the pan. Let the mixture cook for about 1 minute.

3. Gently lift the edge of the pancake to see if it is browned. Once browned, turn the pancake with a slotted turner, or toss and then cook the other side.

4. Serve with lemon juice and sugar, ice cream, maple syrup, golden syrup, or fruit, such as strawberries.

BEEF CHIMICHURI

EASE
★★★★☆

SERVES
4

PREP
20 MINS

COOK
45 MINS

If you were being picky, and wanted an authentic Chimichuri, you wouldn't use coriander in the dressing, but we just prefer it to parsley. Your call.

4 medium **potatoes**, cut into wedges

2 tablespoons **olive oil**

3 tablespoons **olive oil**

1 teaspoon **cumin**

1 teaspoon **coriander**

1 teaspoon **paprika**

4 **rump steaks**

DRESSING

1/2 clove **garlic**, finely chopped

3 tablespoons freshly chopped **coriander** or **flat leaf parsley**

3 tablespoons **white wine vinegar**

3 tablespoons **olive oil**

1 Preheat the oven to 180C° fan/200°C/gas 6.

2 Put the potato wedges on a roasting tray. Mix with the oil and season with salt and pepper. Place in the oven for 45 minutes.

3 Mix the olive oil, cumin, coriander and paprika in a large bowl. Season with salt and pepper. Add the beef steaks and mix in with the spices.

4 Meanwhile, mix together the dressing ingredients.

5 15 minutes before the end of the cooking time for the wedges, heat a frying pan and fry the steaks, on a fairly high heat, for 2 minutes each side. Turn down the heat and fry for a further 2 minutes each side for rare beef, 4 minutes each side for medium rare.

6 Leave the steak to rest for a couple of minutes and then slice.

7 Serve with the dressing and the wedges.

SCAN ME

For more desserts that will wow your friends

£1.84 /PERSON

BEEF IN ALE WITH CHEDDAR & MUSTARD MASH

EASE
★★★☆☆

When mashing potatoes, don't beat them to a pulp, as they go 'gloopy'. Just mash until the lumps have gone.

SERVES 6

PREP
20 MINS

COOK
90 MINS

1 tablespoon **olive oil**

2 **onions**, cut into wedges

1kg **cubed stewing beef**

2 tablespoons **flour**

500ml bottle **ale**

2 **beef stock cubes**

12 **carrots**, peeled and chopped

10 medium **potatoes**, peeled (optional) and cut into chunks

25g **butter**, measure using packet

1 mug grated **Cheddar cheese**

1 tablespoon **wholegrain mustard**

1 Preheat the oven to 180°C fan/200°C/gas 6.

2 Heat the oil in a large pan or wok and fry the onions until they begin to brown. Add the meat and fry until the meat is no longer pink.

3 Add the flour and stir well. Add the ale and stock and bring to the boil. Season well with salt and pepper. The sauce should thicken.

4 Transfer to a casserole dish and cover with a lid or foil. Cook in the oven for 1¹/₂ hours. After 1 hour, give it a stir to make sure it is not sticking to the bottom of the dish. Add a little more water if the sauce is getting too thick.

5 15 minutes before the end of the cooking time, put the carrots in boiling, salted water and simmer for 10 minutes. Once cooked, drain and return to the pan until needed.

6 Put the potatoes into boiling, salted water and simmer for 10 minutes until tender. Drain and return to the pan. Add the butter, cheese and mustard and mash.

7 Serve.

SCAN ME

Let your cooker do the work. See other similar recipes

£1.70 /PERSON

EASE ★☆☆☆☆

SERVES 2-3

PREP 25 MINS

V OPTION

CHUNKY CHICKEN WITH APPLES AND CIDER

If you want to use normal onions rather than spring onions, fry them in the oil before you add the chicken pieces.

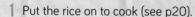

1 mug **basmati rice**

1 tablespoon **olive oil**

2 **chicken breasts**, cut into chunks or 200g **Quorn pieces**

4 **spring onions**, chopped

2 **red apples**, cored and cut into chunks

1½ mugs (450ml) **cider**

½ **chicken** or **veg stock cube**

½ mug (150ml) **double cream**

1 teaspoon **dried basil**

1 Put the rice on to cook (see p20).

2 Meanwhile, heat the oil in a frying pan. Add the chicken and fry for 1–2 minutes, until no longer pink. Add the spring onions and apple and cook for 1 minute. Season with salt and pepper. Add the cider and stock. Keep on a high heat to reduce the cider for around 5 minutes.

3 Add the cream and basil. Bring to the boil and take off the heat straight away. Using fresh basil is best, but not essential.

4 Serve with the rice.

SPICY LAMB CASSEROLE

£2.35 /PERSON

Lamb is a bit pricey, but makes a good treat when friends are around.

EASE
★★☆☆☆

SERVES
6

PREP
20 MINS

COOK
90 MINS

1 tablespoon **olive oil**

2 **onions**, sliced

1 clove **garlic**, finely chopped

750g **stewing lamb**, cut into cubes

2 x 400g tin **chopped tomatoes**

1 **fat red chilli**, chopped

1 tablespoon **tomato purée**

400g tin **chickpeas**, rinsed and drained

1 tablespoon **ground coriander**

8 medium **potatoes**, peeled and cut into chunks

25g **butter**, measure using packet

300g **green beans**, trimmed

1 Preheat the oven to 180°C fan/200°C/gas 6.

2 Heat the oil in a large pan. Fry the onions and garlic for 3–4 minutes, until the onions begin to soften.

3 Add the lamb and cook until the meat is no longer pink and beginning to brown. Season with salt and pepper.

4 Add the rest of the ingredients and bring to the boil.

5 Transfer the contents of the pan to a casserole dish and place in the oven for 1¹/₂–2 hours. Stir a couple of times.

6 When the casserole is 15 minutes from the end of the cooking time, boil the potatoes (see p18). Drain, add the butter and mash.

7 Serve the casserole with the mash and cooked green beans (see p18).

£0.94 /PERSON

EASE
★★★★☆

SERVES
4

PREP
10 MINS

COOK
35 MINS

V

CORNBREAD

The perfect accompaniment to a 'chilli', such as the one opposite.

1 ⅓ mugs **fine polenta**

½ mug **plain flour**

2 teaspoons **bicarbonate soda**

½ teaspoon **salt**

1 mug grated **Cheddar cheese**

100g **feta**, crumbled

1 **egg**

1 ⅓ mugs (400ml) **buttermilk**

1 **red onion**, cut into thin wedges

100g **feta**

2 tablespoons **sesame seeds**

1 Preheat the oven to 180°c fan/200°C/gas 6. Grease and line a traybake tin (approx. 30x20cm).

2 Mix together the dry ingredients, including the first 100g of feta.

3 Beat the egg and mix with the buttermilk. Add to the dry ingredients, season with salt and pepper, and gently stir.

4 Pour into the tin and spread out. Push the onion wedges into the cornbread along with the remaining feta. Sprinkle with sesame seeds.

5 Bake in the oven for 35 minutes.

6 Now make the chilli opposite.

CHILLI BEEF

You can eat this with the cornbread opposite, or with some rice.

£0.88 /PERSON

EASE
★★☆☆☆

SERVES 4

PREP 20 MINS

V OPTION

2 tablespoons **olive oil**

1 **red pepper**, chopped

1 **onion**, sliced

3 cloves **garlic**, chopped

500g **beef** or **Quorn mince**

400g tin **chopped tomatoes**

400g tin **red kidney beans**, rinsed and drained

400g tin **black-eyed beans**, rinsed and drained

1 **fat red chilli**, chopped

1 teaspoon **cumin**

1 teaspoon **coriander**

1/2 mug **water**

1 tablespoon **tomato purée**

1/2 teaspoon **chilli powder**

bread or **cornbread**, see opposite to serve

1 Heat the oil in a large frying pan or wok. Add the pepper, onion and garlic and fry for 2 minutes.

2 Add the mince and fry until no longer pink.

3 Add the rest of the ingredients, season with salt and pepper, and simmer for 10 minutes.

4 Serve with the cornbread opposite.

£1.11 /PERSON

BACON-WRAPPED MEATLOAF

EASE
★★★★★

SERVES
5-6

PREP
20 MINS

COOK
135 MINS

COOL
2 HRS

You do need a loaf tin for this recipe. The meat loaf can be prepared ahead of time, giving time to relax before your friends arrive.

MEATLOAF

8 slices **streaky bacon**

1kg **beef mince**

1 **onion**, finely chopped

1 **egg**, beaten

1 teaspoon **dried basil**

5 pieces **sun-dried tomatoes**, finely chopped

DRESSING

1 tablespoon **olive oil**

1 teaspoon **wholegrain mustard**

1 tablespoon **white wine vinegar**

1 teaspoon **sugar**

salt and **pepper**

4–5 large **potatoes**

salad

1 Preheat the oven to 180°C fan/200°C/gas 6.

2 Lightly grease and line a 1lb loaf tin with greaseproof paper. Lightly grease the paper and line the tin with the streaky bacon.

3 Mix the rest of the meatloaf ingredients together in a bowl. Season well with salt and pepper. Place in the loaf tin, making sure that the bacon stays on the outside. See photo.

4 Place in the oven for 75 minutes. Take out and leave to cool for at least 2 hours.

5 One hour before you plan to eat, make incisions in the tops of the potatoes, drizzle with olive oil, and put in the oven to bake for 50–60 minutes.

6 Mix the dressing ingredients together. Pour over the salad just before serving.

7 Once the loaf is cool, slice with a sharp knife and serve with the potatoes and salad.

SCAN ME

For more beef recipes

BEEF BURGERS

Beef burgers don't have to be unhealthy. Make them yourself from good quality mince.

EASE
★★★☆☆

SERVES
2

PREP
5 MINS

COOK
10 MINS

V

250g **beef mince**

1 **egg**, beaten

1 tablespoon **olive oil**

2 **bread buns**

any combination of **lettuce, gherkin tomatoes, cucumber**, etc.

mayo, tomato sauce or **mustard**

potatoes for wedges

1 If you want to serve these burgers with potato wedges, begin cooking them first (see p152).

2 Mix the mince and half the egg together. Season well with salt and pepper.

3 Divide the mixture into 2 and shape the burgers about 2cm thick.

4 Heat the oil in a frying pan and gently fry the burgers on each side for 4–5 minutes, or until nicely browned and cooked through.

5 Serve in bread buns with salad.

6 Serve with potato wedges.

LASAGNE

Once you have mastered Spaghetti Bolognese and the Quick Cheese Sauce, try this recipe when you have a few friends around.

£1.01 /PERSON

EASE ★★★★★

SERVES 4

PREP 25 MINS

COOK 25 MINS

V OPTION

QUICK CHEESE SAUCE

2 mugs grated **Cheddar cheese**

3 tablespoons **flour**

2 mugs **milk**

25g **butter**, measure using packet

salt and **pepper**

1/2 teaspoon **nutmeg**

BOLOGNESE SAUCE

1 tablespoon **olive oil**

1 **onion**, chopped

2 cloves **garlic**, finely chopped

500g **beef** or **Quorn mince**

400g tin **chopped tomatoes**

2 tablespoons **tomato purée**

1 **beef** or **veg stock cube**

1 teaspoon **mixed herbs**

250g packet **lasagne sheets**

1/2 mug grated **Cheddar cheese**

1 Preheat the oven to 180°C fan/200°C/gas 6.

2 Make the Cheese Sauce (see p31). Add the nutmeg and stir.

3 Make the Bolognese Sauce (see p67), minus mushrooms.

4 Using an oblong casserole dish, put a layer of Bolognese sauce on the bottom of the dish and cover with some lasagne sheets, making sure they do not overlap. Next, put a layer of cheese sauce, then pasta sheets, then the rest of the Bolognese sauce. Lay more pasta sheets and then the rest of the cheese sauce. Top with grated cheese.

5 Cook for 25 minutes. Test the pasta with a fork to see if it is cooked through. If it is not, cook for another 5–10 minutes.

6 Serve with salad or garlic bread (see p24).

£1.95 /PERSON

EASE
★★☆☆☆

SERVES
2

PREP
15 MINS

V OPTION

BUFFALO CHICKEN WRAP

Using Tabasco, or hot sauce, is such a simple way of instantly adding spicy heat that is packed with flavour.

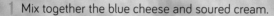

50g **blue cheese**, crumbled

¹/₄ mug (75ml) **soured cream**

1 tablespoon **olive oil**

2 **chicken breasts**, cut into strips or 200g **Quorn pieces**

hot sauce or **Tabasco** (as much as you can handle!)

4 **soft tortillas**

¹/₂ **Romaine lettuce**, sliced

1 stick **celery**, sliced

1 Mix together the blue cheese and soured cream.

2 Heat the oil in a frying pan and add the chicken. Fry until lightly browned and cooked through. Season with salt and pepper.

3 Add the hot sauce and cook for 1 minute.

4 Divide everything between the tortillas. Add more hot sauce if you like things spicy.

150 friends around

BEEF TACOS

£0.90 /PERSON

Fun food, best served and eaten straight away. Prop the taco shells up against each other to keep them upright.

EASE
★★★☆☆

SERVES 4

PREP 30 MINS

V OPTION

1 tablespoon **olive oil**

1 **onion**, chopped

2 cloves **garlic**, finely chopped

500g **beef** or **Quorn mince**

1 teaspoon **chilli powder**

1 teaspoon **paprika**

400g tin **red kidney beans**, rinsed and drained

2 tablespoons **tomato purée**

2 **tomatoes**, chopped

1 **beef** or **veg stock cube**

1/4 mug **water**

SALSA

5cm **cucumber**, cut into small cubes

2 **tomatoes**, chopped

1 small **red onion**, chopped

juice of 1/2 **lemon**

1 tablespoon **olive oil**

salt and **pepper**

1/2 teaspoon **paprika**

8 **taco shells**

2 **Little Gem lettuces**

soured cream

1. Preheat the oven to 180°C fan/200°C/gas 6.

2. Heat the oil in a frying pan or wok, fry the onions and garlic, until the onions begin to soften. Add the meat and cook until no longer pink. Add the rest of the ingredients, season with salt and pepper, and simmer for 10 minutes.

3. Mix the salsa ingredients together.

4. Meanwhile, put the taco shells in the oven for 5 minutes.

5. Arrange everything in the taco shells.

friends around **151**

£0.44 /PERSON

EASE
★★☆☆☆

SERVES 1

PREP 5 MINS

COOK 35 MINS

V OPTION

POTATO WEDGES AND DIPS

This is excellent party or movie night food, easy to make and pretty much infinitely scalable!

2 medium **potatoes**	1 tablespoon **olive oil**

CHOOSE ONE OF THESE OPTIONAL FLAVOURINGS AND MIX WITH THE OIL

1 clove **garlic**, finely chopped	1 teaspoon **paprika**
1 teaspoon **rosemary**	1/4 teaspoon **curry powder**

1. Preheat the oven to 200°C fan/220°C/gas 7.
2. Cut the potatoes into thin 'wedges'.
3. Put the potatoes on a baking tray or caserole dish. Sprinkle with the oil (either just olive oil, or the options above). Using your hands, toss the potatoes in the oil, making sure that every piece of potato is covered. Separate the wedges, sitting them on their 'backs'. This leaves all the flat surfaces open to brown.
4. Season well with salt and pepper.
5. Cook for 35–40 minutes in the oven, until the potatoes are crisp and browned.

Turns out, describing how to cut wedges isn't that easy.
So Joy made a video to show you how it's done.

DIPS

These can be used if you have a party. Use carrot sticks, celery sticks, spicy crisps cheese straws, or the potato wedges on the opposite page.

EASE
★☆☆☆☆

SERVES
1+

PREP
10 MINS

V

CHEESY MUSTARD £0.78 TOTAL

½ mug (150ml) **soured cream**
½ mug finely grated **cheese**
1 teaspoon **wholegrain mustard**

MINTY YOGURT £0.58 TOTAL

½ x 400ml pot **natural yogurt**
¼ **cucumber**, chopped
1 small **onion**, finely chopped
1 teaspoon **dried mint**

SOURED CREAM AND ONIONS £0.86 TOTAL

½ mug (150ml) **soured cream**
1 clove **garlic**, very finely chopped
2 **spring onions**, finely chopped
juice of ½ a **lemon**

SPICY TOMATO £0.58 TOTAL

½ mug (150ml) **crème fraîche**
2 teaspoons **tomato purée**
3–4 drops **Tabasco sauce**

LIME YOGURT £0.66 TOTAL

½ x 400ml pot **natural yogurt**
3 tablespoons **mayo**
grated rind and juice of a **lime**

CHEESE AND ONION £1.28 TOTAL

½ mug (150ml) **soured cream**
5–6 spring **onions**, chopped
½ mug finely grated **cheese**
1 teaspoon **dried chives**
salt and **pepper**

CHEESE AND CHILLI £0.61 TOTAL

½ x 300g pack **cream cheese**
1 tablespoon **chilli dipping sauce**
2 tablespoons **crème fraîche**

IT'S SO EASY..

...with each of these, just mix together and season with salt and pepper!

£0.32 /PERSON

EASE
★☆☆☆☆

SERVES
2-3

PREP
5 MINS

COOK
2 MINS

V

NACHOS

Nachos are so quick to make and are excellent for parties, or snacks, while you are relaxing or watching a film, etc.

½ x 200g packet **tortilla chips**

1½ mugs grated **Cheddar cheese**

Dipping Salsa sauce (see next page)

1 Preheat the oven to 220°C fan/240°C/gas 9.

2 If you are going to make the salsa, make it now (see next page).

3 Pile the chips on an ovenproof dish and cover with the grated cheese.

4 Place in the oven until all the cheese looks like it has melted. The cheese only needs to melt, it does not need to brown.

5 Pour the salsa over the top, serve and eat immediately.

SALSA

If you are having a party, these will work out much cheaper than the bought variety. Salsa is good with tortilla chips, quesadillas and big wraps. If you like your salsa really hot, then adjust the amount of chilli powder or chilli flakes.

TOMATO AND ONION SALSA

£1.27 TOTAL

4 **tomatoes**, cut into small pieces

1 **green chilli**, finely chopped

1 small **onion**, finely chopped

1 teaspoon **sugar**

1 teaspoon **lemon juice**

salt and **pepper**

DIPPING SALSA

£0.77 TOTAL

1 tablespoon **olive oil**

1 **onion**, finely chopped

3 cloves **garlic**, finely chopped

400g tin **chopped tomatoes**

1/2 tablespoon **tomato purée**

1 teaspoon **chilli flakes**

1/2 teaspoon **paprika**

1 teaspoon **sugar**

2 teaspoons **dried chives**

AVOCADO SALSA

£1.37 TOTAL

1 medium **avocado**, peeled and chopped into small pieces

1 medium **onion**, finely chopped

2 medium **tomatoes**, roughly chopped

1/2 teaspoon **chilli powder**

1/4 teaspoon **paprika**

1/2 teaspoon **sugar**

1 teaspoon **lemon juice** (this stops the avocado from discolouring)

salt and **pepper**

For Avocado Salsa and Tomato and Onion Salsa, simply prepare the ingredients and mix together. For the dipping salsa, follow these steps.

1. Heat the oil in a saucepan and fry the onions and garlic until they begin to brown.

2. Add the chopped tomatoes, tomato purée, chilli, paprika, chives and sugar and bring to the boil. Simmer gently for 3–4 minutes.

CHICKEN DRUMSTICKS AND WEDGES

£1.09 /PERSON

EASE
★★☆☆☆

SERVES
3

PREP
10 MINS

COOK
40 MINS

Look out for bargain offers in the supermarket and buy a big bag of drumsticks; they will always come in handy.

1 teaspoon **mustard**

1 tablespoon **tomato sauce**

1 tablespoon **Worcestershire sauce**

salt and **pepper**

1 teaspoon **brown sugar**

1kg **chicken drumsticks**

3 medium **potatoes**

2 tablespoons **olive oil**

1 Preheat the oven to 180°C fan/200°C/gas 6.

2 Mix together the mustard, tomato sauce, Worcestershire sauce, salt, pepper and sugar.

3 Cover the chicken legs with half the sauce.

4 Place on an oiled baking tray or casserole dish. Bake for 20 minutes. Cover the legs with the rest of the liquid and bake for another 20 minutes.

5 While the drumsticks are cooking, cut the potatoes into wedges (see p134), place on a baking tray and sprinkle with the oil, salt and pepper. Bake in the oven for 30–35 minutes.

TOASTADAS WITH AVOCADO SALSA

£1.21 /PERSON

2 **soft tortillas**, cut into wedges

1 tablespoon **olive oil**

2 **onions**, sliced

1 **green chilli**, finely chopped

400g tin **chickpeas**, rinsed and drained

1 tablespoon **tomato purée**

1 teaspoon **Tabasco sauce**

1 tablespoon **crème fraîche**

4 **tomatoes**, sliced

2 mugs grated **Cheddar cheese**

SALSA

3 **tomatoes**, chopped

1 **green chilli**, finely chopped

1 **avocado**, peeled and cut into chunks

4 **spring onions**, sliced

juice of a **lemon**

2 tablespoons **olive oil**

EASE ★★★★☆

SERVES 4-5

PREP 25 MINS

COOK 10 MINS

V

1. Preheat the oven to 200°C fan/220°C/gas 7.

2. Place the tortilla wedges on a non-stick baking tray.

3. Heat the oil in a frying pan and fry the onions and chilli until the onions begin to brown. Add the chickpeas, tomato purée and Tabasco sauce and heat through. Blitz with a hand-held blender, or mash with a potato masher or fork; it doesn't need to be really smooth. Add the crème fraîche and salt and pepper to taste.

4. Divide the mixture between each wedge of tortilla. Top with the sliced tomatoes and the grated cheese.

5. Place in the oven for 8–10 minutes until browned.

6. Mix the salsa ingredients together and serve with the toastadas.

£ 1.37 /PERSON

EASE
★★★★☆

SERVES
4

PREP
25 MINS

COOK
30 MINS

V OPTION

MOUSSAKA

This dish can be quite rich, so serving with the green salad is a good option. For those with good appetites, serve with baked potatoes.

1 tablespoon **olive oil**	1 tablespoon **olive oil**
1 large **onion**, sliced	1 large **aubergine**
1 clove **garlic**, finely chopped	25g **butter**, measure using packet
500g **lamb** or **Quorn mince**	1 tablespoon **flour**
1 **veg stock cube**, crumbled	1 mug **milk**
400g tin **chopped tomatoes**	1/2 teaspoon **paprika**
1 tablespoon **tomato purée**	**green salad** or **baked potato** (see p22) to serve

1 Preheat the oven to 180°C fan/200°C/gas 6.

2 Heat the oil in a frying pan and fry the onions until they become soft. Add the garlic and mince and fry until the mince is no longer pink. If you are having baked potatoes, put them in the oven now.

3 Add the stock cube, tomatoes and tomato purée, bring to the boil and then turn down to simmer for 10 minutes. Season well with salt and pepper and put in the bottom of a casserole dish.

4 Cut the aubergine into 1cm slices. Heat the oil in a frying pan and fry the slices for 1 minute each side. Put them on top of the mince in the casserole dish.

5 Heat the butter in a small saucepan, add the flour and stir well. Take off the heat and add the milk. Mix well and return to the heat. Gently bring to the boil, stirring frequently, the sauce should thicken. Add the paprika and pour over the top of the aubergines.

6 Place in the oven for 25–30 minutes until the top is browned. Serve with the green salad or baked potatoes.

CHICKEN WITH PESTO PASTA

£1.66 /PERSON

EASE
★★☆☆☆

SERVES
4

PREP
30 MINS

2 mugs **pasta** (we used fusilli)

1 tablespoon **olive oil**

3 **chicken breasts**

1 **onion**, sliced

2 cloves **garlic**, finely chopped

1 **red pepper**, sliced

20 **black olives**, roughly chopped

400g pack **cherry tomatoes**, halved

DRESSING

2 tablespoons **olive oil**

2 tablespoons **green pesto**

juice of a **lemon**

salt and **pepper**

200g pack **feta cheese**

1 Put the pasta on to cook (see p21). Drain and return to pan.

2 Heat the oil in a frying pan and add the chicken breasts. Season with salt and pepper. Cook on a high heat for 2 minutes each side. Turn down the heat and cook, with the lid on, for a further 4 minutes each side. Set aside. Once cooled slightly, thinly slice.

3 Fry the onions, garlic and pepper until soft. Season with salt and pepper. Add the olives and tomatoes to the pan and take off the heat.

4 Add the cooked chicken and pasta to the pan and mix together.

5 Drizzle with the combined dressing ingredients and crumble the feta over the top.

MAKE YOUR OWN TAKEAWAYS

Tired of shelling out loads of dosh on takeaways? Make your own for a fraction of the price, plus you know exactly what's in it!

SWEET AND SOUR CHICKEN

You definitely need to use chicken breast in this recipe, as thighs and legs will not cook in the time.

£1.64 /PERSON

EASE
★★☆☆☆

SERVES 2

PREP 20 MINS

V OPTION

1 mug **basmati rice**

SWEET AND SOUR SAUCE

2 tablespoons **tomato purée**

3 tablespoons **sugar**

2 tablespoons **white wine vinegar**

1 tablespoon **soy sauce**

1 dessertspoon **cornflour**

1 mug **water**

1 tablespoon **olive oil**

1 **onion**, chopped

1 clove **garlic**, finely chopped

4 **mushrooms**, sliced

1/2 **red pepper**, sliced

2 **chicken breasts**, cut into chunks or 200g **Quorn pieces**

227g tin **pineapple slices**, drained and cut into chunks

1 Put the rice on to cook (see p20).

2 Meanwhile, thoroughly mix all the sauce ingredients in a saucepan. Once combined, gently bring to the boil. The sauce should thicken. Remove from the heat and set to one side.

3 Heat the oil in a frying pan and fry the onion, garlic, mushrooms and pepper for 1 minute. Add the chicken and cook until no longer pink.

4 Add the sweet and sour sauce and pineapple to the pan. Bring to the boil, turn down and simmer for 3 minutes.

5 Serve with rice.

£1.44 /PERSON

EASE ★★☆☆☆

SERVES 2

PREP 25 MINS

V OPTION

CHICKEN CURRY

If you use chicken thighs in this recipe, precook them in the oven for 50 minutes in a casserole dish with a little water and salt and pepper.

1 mug **basmati rice**

1 tablespoon **olive oil**

1 **onion**, chopped

3 cloves **garlic**, finely chopped

1 **potato**, cut into chunks

2 **chicken breasts**, cut into chunks or 200g **Quorn pieces**

1 dessertspoon **flour**

³/₄ mug **water**

1 tablespoon **mild curry paste** (use less if the curry paste is hot)

1 **chicken** or **veg stock cube**, crumbled

¹/₂ mug **natural yogurt**

1 Put the rice on to cook (see p20).

2 Heat the oil in a wok and fry the onion, garlic and potato.

3 Add the chicken and cook for 2–3 minutes until the chicken is no longer pink on the outside. Season well with salt and pepper.

4 Add the flour and stir well. Add the water, curry paste and stock cube. Bring to the boil and then simmer for 7–8 minutes until the chicken and the vegetables are cooked.

5 Stir in the yogurt. Cook gently for 1 minute.

LEMON CHICKEN

This dish is incredibly easy to make and tastes delicious. This recipe will cost a fraction of the price you would pay for a 'takeaway'.

£1.44 /PERSON

EASE ★★★☆☆

SERVES 2

PREP 25 MINS

1 mug **basmati rice**

1 tablespoon **olive oil**

2 **chicken breasts**

½ **lemon**, cut into slices

2 **spring onions**, thinly sliced

SAUCE

1 dessertspoon **cornflour**

¾ mug **cold water**

juice of a **lemon**

2 tablespoons **sugar**

1 Put the rice on to cook (see p20).

2 Heat the oil in the frying pan. Add the chicken breasts. Season well with salt and pepper. Cook on a high heat for 2 minutes each side. Turn down and cook on a low heat, with the lid on, for a further 4 minutes each side. Remove from the heat and set to one side.

3 In a saucepan, mix together the sauce ingredients until smooth.

4 Once combined, gently bring to the boil. It should thicken. Add the slices of lemon and gently heat for 1 minute.

5 Slice the chicken breasts and serve with the sauce and spring onions.

SCAN ME

We've done a video tutorial on how to pan-fry a chicken breast.

CHICKEN NOODLES

This is nearly as quick as pot noodle, but much more nutritious and appetizing.

1 tablespoon **olive oil**

1 **chicken breast**, cut chunks
or 100g **Quorn pieces**

2 **spring onions**, sliced

1/2 **red pepper**, chopped

1/2 **chicken** or **veg stock cube**,
dissolved in 1/2 mug **hot water**

1 tablespoon **soy sauce**

150g pack **straight-to-wok egg
noodles**

1 Heat the oil in a frying pan and fry the chicken until it is no longer
   pink. Season with salt and pepper.

2 Add the onion and pepper and fry for 1 minute.

3 Add the stock, soy sauce and noodles and cook for 1 minute.

4 Serve.

PORK NOODLE STIR-FRY

£1.51 /PERSON

EASE
★★☆☆☆

SERVES
2-3

PREP
25 MINS

It is best to use fresh egg noodles, but the ready-to-wok ones are fine. Cut the pork very thinly, fry quickly and it will stay tender.

SAUCE

3 tablespoons **soy sauce**

2 tablespoons **white wine vinegar**

1 tablespoon **honey**

1 tablespoon freshly grated **ginger**

juice of a **lemon**

1 teaspoon **cornflour**

1/3 mug **water**

2 tablespoons **olive oil**

2 medium-sized **pork steaks**, thinly sliced

1/2 **red pepper**, thinly sliced

100g **mangetout**, sliced lengthways

6 **spring onions**, sliced

2 **mushrooms**, sliced

200g pack **fresh egg noodles**

1 Mix together the sauce ingredients. Set aside until needed.

2 Heat the oil in a wok and add the pork slices. Stir-fry for 3–4 minutes. Add the peppers, mangetout, onions and mushrooms. Cook for a further 2–3 minutes.

3 Add the sauce and bring to the boil, stirring frequently. The sauce should thicken.

4 Add the noodles and heat through for 1 minute.

5 Serve.

£1.57 /PERSON

 EASE
★★☆☆☆

 SERVES 2

 PREP 15 MINS

SPICY PRAWNS

It is not recommended that you reheat prawns, so if you make enough for 2 people, it is best to share with a friend.

1 mug **basmati rice**

1 tablespoon **olive oil**

1 small **onion**, finely chopped

1 clove **garlic**, chopped very finely

200g tin **chopped tomatoes**

1 dessertspoon **tomato purée**

1 teaspoon **curry paste**

200g **peeled, cooked prawns**, drained

¼ teaspoon **dried basil**

1 Put the rice on to cook (see p20).

2 Heat the oil in a frying pan and fry the onion and garlic until the onions begin to brown.

3 Add the chopped tomatoes, tomato purée and curry paste and bring to the boil. Cook for 2–3 minutes.

4 Add the prawns, basil and season with salt and pepper. Cook for 1–2 minutes.

5 Serve with the rice.

CHICKEN TERIYAKI STIR-FRY

£1.70 /PERSON

Stir-fry using a high heat. That way you get some colour on your chicken and veg without overcooking them. You still want your veg to have a little crunch.

EASE ★★☆☆☆

1 mug **basmati rice**

1 tablespoon **olive oil**

1 small **onion**, sliced

1 clove **garlic**, finely chopped

1 **fat red chilli**, thinly sliced

1/2 **green pepper**, thinly sliced

2 **chicken breast**, cut into chunks or 200g **Quorn pieces**

6 tablespoons **teriyaki sauce**

2 teaspoons **sugar**

200g **bean sprouts**

SERVES 2-3

PREP 20 MINS

V OPTION

1 Put the rice on to cook (see p20).

2 Heat the oil in a wok. Add the onions, garlic, chilli and peppers. Stir-fry on a high heat for 1 minute. Add the chicken and cook until no longer pink, stirring frequently. Season with salt and pepper.

3 Add the teriyaki sauce and sugar to the wok and bring to the boil. Add the bean sprouts and stir-fry for 1 minute.

4 Serve with the rice.

EASY MONGOLIAN BEEF

£1.79 /PERSON

EASE ★★★☆☆

SERVES 2

PREP 15 MINS

1 mug **basmati rice**

2 tablespoons **olive oil**

200g **rump steak**, sliced

6 **spring onions**, sliced

1 clove **garlic**, finely chopped

1 tablespoon freshly grated **ginger**

2 teaspoons **cornflour**

1/2 mug **water**

2 tablespoons **soy sauce**

2 tablespoons **brown sugar**

1 Put the rice on to cook (see p20).

2 Heat the oil in a large frying pan or wok. Add the beef and fry on a high heat until lightly browned.

3 Remove from the pan and set to one side. Add the onions, garlic and ginger to the pan and fry for 30 seconds.

4 Mix together the cornflour, water, soy and sugar, add to the pan and bring to the boil. Return the beef to the pan.

5 Cook for 1 minute on a medium heat.

6 Serve with the rice.

THAI COCONUT NOODLES

£1.62
/PERSON

EASE
★★☆☆☆

SERVES
2

PREP
15 MINS

V

100g **dried rice noodles**

1 tablespoon **olive oil**

125g **mushrooms**, sliced

4 **spring onions**, sliced

200ml tin **coconut milk**

1 tablespoon **Thai red curry paste**

75g **sugar snaps**, sliced

1 tablespoon **soy sauce**

juice of ½ **lime**

100g packet **unsalted peanuts**

2 tablespoons freshly chopped **coriander** (optional)

1   Put the noodles in a large bowl and cover with boiling water. Leave for 8–10 minutes, or until tender, and drain.

2   Meanwhile, heat the oil in a wok. Add the mushrooms and spring onions and fry for 1 minute.

3   Add the coconut milk and curry paste and bring to the boil.

4   Add the rest of the ingredients, apart from the coriander, and quickly heat through.

5   Stir in the cooked noodles and coriander.

£0.63 /PERSON

EASE
★★☆☆☆

SERVES
4

PREP
20 MINS

OPTION

MINI MUFFIN PIZZAS

There are a variety of toppings here for you to try.

BASIC TOMATO SAUCE

1 tablespoon **olive oil**

1 small **onion**, chopped

1 clove **garlic**, finely chopped

200g tin **chopped tomatoes**

1 tablespoon **tomato purée**

1 teaspoon **sugar**

1 teaspoon **dried mixed herbs**

salt and **pepper**

TOPPING OPTIONS

pepperoni or **salami, sun-dried tomatoes, mushrooms and peppers**

ham, pineapple and **peppers**

tuna and **sweetcorn**

sun-dried tomatoes and **anchovies**

sun-dried tomatoes, mushrooms and olives

4 **muffins**

250g **mozzarella cheese**, torn apart, or 1 mug grated **Cheddar cheese**

1 Heat the oil in a frying pan and fry the onions and garlic until the onions begin to brown. Add the rest of the sauce ingredients, bring to the boil and simmer for 2–3 minutes.

2 Preheat the grill.

3 Halve the muffins. Divide the tomato sauce between the muffins.

4 Arrange the various toppings on the muffins and top with whatever cheese you are using.

5 Transfer the muffins to the grill pan. Cook under the grill until the cheese begins to bubble and brown.

DATE-NIGHT

Need to impress that special someone without slogging in the kitchen for hours? Try some of these.

SALMON STEAK WITH COCONUT RICE

Salmon is a little expensive, but wait for it to come on offer at the supermarket, buy in bulk and freeze some.

£3.09 /PERSON

EASE
★★★☆☆

SERVES 2

PREP 35 MINS

400ml tin **coconut milk**

²/₃ mug **water**

1 mug **basmati rice**

100g **green beans**, trimmed

4 **anchovy fillets**, chopped

1 teaspoon **dried basil**

2 tablespoons **mayo**

1 tablespoon **olive oil**

2 **salmon steaks**

1 In a saucepan, bring the coconut milk and water to the boil. Add the rice and stir. Simmer gently, with a lid on the pan, for 10 minutes.

2 Cook the green beans in simmering water for about 6–8 minutes, drain and return to the pan.

3 Meanwhile, make the sauce by mixing the chopped, anchovy fillets, basil and mayo. Season well with salt and pepper and set aside.

4 Heat the oil in a frying pan. Add the salmon steaks and cook on a high heat for 2 minutes each side. If the steak is approximately 2–3cm thick, you will need to cook for a further 5 minutes on a low heat. With the point of a sharp knife, gently push the flesh of the fish apart to check that it is cooked through. For smaller steaks, reduce the time accordingly.

5 Serve with the rice, green beans and the sauce.

£2.85 /PERSON

EASE
★★★★☆

SERVES
2

PREP
20 MINS

COOK
35 MINS

CAJUN CHICKEN WITH WEDGES AND SALSA

Remember to keep your knife sharp, so that when you cut the chicken, you get good, clean cuts.

3–4 medium **potatoes**

1 tablespoon **olive oil**

2 tablespoons **Cajun chicken seasoning**

2 **chicken breasts**

1 tablespoon **olive oil**

SALSA

1 medium **avocado**, cut into small pieces

200g tin **sweetcorn**, drained

3 **tomatoes**, cut into small chunks

3 **spring onions**, chopped

1 **fat red chilli**, thinly sliced

1 tablespoon **olive oil**

juice of ¹/₂ **lemon**

1 teaspoon **sugar**

1 Preheat the oven to 180°C fan/200°C/gas 6.

2 Cut the potatoes into wedges and place on a baking sheet. Drizzle with the oil and season with salt and pepper. Mix with your hands to distribute the oil evenly. Stand the wedges up, and apart from each other, so they brown on all sides. Put in the oven for 30–35 minutes.

3 Put the Cajun seasoning on a plate. Press the chicken breasts into the seasoning and coat them well.

4 Heat the oil in a frying pan, add the chicken breasts and cook, on a high heat, for 2 minutes each side. Turn down the heat and cook, with the lid on, for a further 4 minutes each side, depending on the size of the chicken breast. Test, by making a cut in the meat, to see that it is no longer pink in the centre. Remove from the pan and slice (see photo).

5 Make the salsa by mixing all the ingredients together.

6 Serve with the chicken, potato wedges and salsa.

SCAN ME

We've done a video tutorial on
how to pan-fry a chicken breast.

£2.80 /PERSON

EASE
★★★☆☆

SERVES
2

PREP
20 MINS

COOK
90 MINS

EASY BEEF STROGANOFF

Avoid being stuck in the kitchen when your date arrives, by cooking this dish ahead of time, leaving only the rice to cook at the last minute.

1 tablespoon **olive oil**

1 **onion**, chopped

2 cloves **garlic**, finely chopped

250g pack **cubed stewing beef**

1 tablespoon **flour**

1 mug **water** or **white wine**

1 **beef stock cube**

1 dessertspoon **wholegrain mustard**

1/4 teaspoon **paprika**

4 **mushrooms**, sliced

1 mug **natural yogurt** or **soured cream**

2 teaspoons **dried basil** or **parsley**

1 mug **basmati rice**

1 Preheat the oven to 160°C fan/180°C/gas 4.

2 Heat the oil in a frying pan and fry the onion and garlic for 1 minute.

3 Add the meat and cook on a medium heat, until the meat is slightly browned, or until the meat is no longer pink.

4 Add the flour and stir well. Add the water or wine, stock cube, mustard, paprika and mushrooms and bring to the boil. Season well.

5 Place in a casserole dish with a lid (or use foil) and put in the oven for 1½ hours. Check every 30 minutes to see that the sauce is not sticking on the bottom of the pan.

6 Remove from the oven. Add the yogurt, or soured cream and parsley.

7 Serve with rice (see p20) and green vegetables (optional).

MEXICAN BEEF

Beef steak is a little expensive, but it is worth buying the best you can so that it is nice and tender.

£1.75 /PERSON

EASE
★★☆☆☆

SERVES
2

PREP
15 MINS

1 mug **basmati rice**

1 tablespoon **olive oil**

1 small **onion**, sliced

1 **carrot**, peeled and thinly sliced

1 clove **garlic**, finely chopped

1/2 **green** or **yellow pepper**, chopped

250g **rump steak**, cut into thin strips

200g tin **chopped tomatoes**

1/2 tablespoon **tomato purée**

1/2 teaspoon **chilli flakes**

1 Put the rice on to cook (see p20).

2 Heat the oil in a frying pan and fry the onions, carrots and garlic for 2–3 minutes, stirring frequently. Add the pepper and cook for a further 2–3 minutes.

3 Add the thinly sliced beef to the pan and cook on a high heat for 2–3 minutes, stirring frequently until the meat is nicely browned.

4 Add the chopped tomatoes, tomato purée and chilli and cook for 2–3 minutes. Season well.

SCAN ME

Joy did a video tutorial of how to make perfect rice every time.

£1.62 /PERSON

 EASE
★★★☆☆

 SERVES 2-3

 PREP 20 MINS

 V OPTION

MANGO CHICKEN

Mango pulp is a bit unusual, but is usually available at supermarkets. If you cannot find it, simply buy a medium-sized mango, peel and slice it, and mash it together with a little water.

1 mug **basmati rice**

1 tablespoon **olive oil**

2 **chicken breasts**, cut into chunks or 200g **Quorn pieces**

5 **spring onions**, chopped

1 clove **garlic**, finely chopped

1 mug (300ml) **tinned mango pulp**

2 teaspoons **curry paste**

1 teaspoon **wholegrain mustard**

1 tablespoon **soured cream**

1 Put the rice on to cook (see p20).

2 Heat the oil in a frying pan and fry the chicken for 2 minutes, then add the onions and garlic. Fry for another 1 minute, stirring continuously. Season with salt and pepper.

3 Add the mango pulp, curry paste and mustard. Simmer for 2–3 minutes over a medium heat.

4 Take the pan off the heat and stir in the soured cream.

5 Serve with the rice.

SCAN ME

Do you want a few more chicken recipes under your belt?

QUESADILLAS

A fun one to share. A little messy to eat so you might want to avoid this one on a first date!? If you are vegetarian, obviously leave out the meat or use Quorn pieces. It is best to buy the soft, flour tortillas.

2 tablespoons **olive oil**

1 **chicken breast**, sliced or 100g **Quorn pieces**

1 **onion**, finely chopped

1 **pepper**, chopped

5 **mushrooms**, sliced

400g tin **cannellini beans**, rinsed and drained

1 tablespoon **tomato purée**

4 tablespoons **water**

25g **butter**, measure using packet

4 **soft tortilla wraps**

avocado salsa (see p155)

1 Heat the oil in a frying pan and fry the chicken until it is no longer pink inside. Take out of the pan and leave to stand.

2 Fry the onion until it begins to brown and then add the pepper and mushrooms. Cook for another 3–4 minutes.

3 Add the chicken, along with the beans, tomato purée and water. Season well with salt and pepper. Remove from the pan and set to one side.

4 If you are making the salsa, make it now (see p155).

5 Preheat the grill.

6 Wash the frying pan. Butter one side of the tortilla wraps. Put the freshly cleaned pan on to heat up. Put one of the wraps, butter side down, in the pan. Put half of the filling onto the wrap and spread it out, then place the other wrap, butter side up, on the top of the filling. Now place under the grill until the butter begins to brown.

7 Slide onto a plate and cut into wedges. Repeat for the second quesadilla. Serve with salsa.

SCAN ME

There are more chicken recipes

CAKES & COOKIES

Looking for some comforting nibbles?
Try a few of these and share them with friends.

RICE KRISPIE CAKES

Mars bars do not melt as quickly as chocolate, so you need to be patient.

£2.09 TOTAL

3 normal size **Mars bars** (58g)
¼ x 250g block **butter**

2 mugs **Rice Krispies**
12 **paper cake cases**

EASE
★☆☆☆☆

MAKES 12

PREP 10 MINS

COOL 15 MINS

V

1 Cut the Mars bars into chunks.

2 Melt the butter slowly in a large pan and then add the chopped up Mars bars. Cook gently over a low heat, stirring frequently. The Mars bars will melt and form a thick, creamy mixture.

3 Add the Rice Krispies and stir quickly.

4 Divide the mixture into the 12 cake cases (use two spoons as the mixture will be quite hot).

5 It is best if you allow them to cool for 15 minutes, but one or two may disappear before then! If they last long enough, you can put them in the fridge.

£1.52 TOTAL

SNICKERDOODLES

Leave the butter out of the fridge for a couple of hours to soften before you try to cream with the sugar.

EASE
★★★☆☆

MAKES
24

PREP
15 MINS

COOK
12 MINS

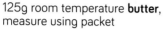

V

125g room temperature **butter**, measure using packet

1/2 mug **granulated sugar**

1 **egg**, beaten

1 teaspoon **vanilla extract**

1 2/3 mugs **self-raising flour**

1/2 teaspoon **nutmeg**

2 tablespoons **granulated sugar**

1 tablespoon **cinnamon**

1 Preheat the oven to 160°C fan/180°C/gas 4. Grease a flat baking tray.

2 Mix the butter and the 1/2 mug of sugar together and beat with a wooden spoon. Add the beaten egg and vanilla. Beat well.

3 Mix in the flour and the nutmeg until the mixture is smooth.

4 Place the 2 tablespoons of sugar and the cinnamon on a plate and mix together.

5 Turn the cookie mixture out onto a surface and squash together. Make into a long sausage, handling as little as possible. Cut into 24. Take each piece and make into a small ball, roll this in the sugar and cinnamon, and place slightly apart on the baking tray.

6 Bake for 12 minutes. The snickerdoodles should be slightly browned.

SCAN ME

For more simple cookie recipes go to

£2.34 TOTAL

CHOCOLATE CHIP COOKIES

These cookies should be crunchy on the outside and a bit 'gooey' on the inside. Don't skimp on the butter and use margarine; it won't taste nearly as good!

125g room temperature **butter**, measure using packet

1 mug **soft brown sugar**

1 large **egg**

1 teaspoon **vanilla extract**

100g packet **chocolate chips**, ½ milk and ½ white works well

1½ mugs **self-raising flour**

1. Preheat the oven to 180°C fan/200°C/gas 6. Grease 2 baking trays. If you only have one tray, you can cook them in two batches. The mixture will be OK to leave half, while the other half cooks.

2. Mix the butter and sugar together and beat well. Add the egg and vanilla extract. Beat well.

3. Add the chocolate chips and mix, then add the flour and mix well. The cookie dough will be quite stiff. Tip onto a floured surface and squash into a long sausage. Do not knead the dough. In fact, handle it as little as possible. Cut into 16 and roll each portion into a ball and then squash until about 1.5cm thick and 6cm across. Place on the baking tray.

4. Put in the oven and bake for 10–12 minutes. The cookies don't need to brown, just be crisp on the outside. Leave a few minutes to cool.

SCAN ME

If you want more friends, make more cookies...simple!
Here are some more simple cookie recipes to try

SCOTCH PANCAKES

You need to keep the pan quite hot for these, but not smoking hot! To make sure they are cooking through in the middle, try one.

2 **eggs**

1/4 mug **brown sugar**

1 mug **self-raising flour**

1/2 mug **water**

white **Flora** or **olive oil** to fry

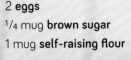

1 Put the eggs, sugar and flour in a bowl and beat with a wooden spoon.

2 Add the water and beat well. The mixture is quite thick.

3 Heat a small amount of white Flora in a frying pan.

4 Put 4 separate dessertspoons of the mixture in the pan and fry until lightly browned. The mixture will rise slightly. Turn the pancakes over and brown the other sides. Repeat with the rest of the mixture.

5 Serve immediately with any combo of butter and jam, honey, maple syrup and ice cream.

£1.27 TOTAL

EASE
★☆☆☆☆

MAKES
18

PREP
5 MINS

COOK
20 MINS

V

FLAP JACKS

Makes good lunch time snacks, along with something a bit more healthy of course!

125g **butter**, measure using packet

3 'heaped' tablespoons **golden syrup**

1/2 mug **soft brown sugar**

2 mugs **rolled oats**

1 Preheat the oven to 170°C fan/190°C/gas 4. Grease a traybake tin (approx. 30x20cm) and put greaseproof paper in the bottom.

2 Put the butter, syrup and sugar in a large pan. Melt gently over a low heat. Do not allow it to boil.

3 Add the oats and mix well.

4 Pour into the baking tray, press down with a spoon and bake in the oven for 20–25 minutes.

5 Leave to cool for about 10 minutes. While the mixture is still warm, and in the baking tray, cut into squares. Should make about 18. Leave in the tin to cool and set.

NICOLE'S NUTTY BROWNIES

Brownies are meant to be soggy on the inside and crisp on the outside, so don't think they are not cooked, or that you have failed, when you sample their delicious soggy centres!

125g **butter**, measure using packet

100g **dark chocolate**

100g pack **chopped, mixed nuts**

1 mug **granulated sugar**

1/2 mug **self-raising flour**

3 large **eggs**, beaten

1 Preheat the oven to 160°C fan/180°C/gas 4.

2 Grease a traybake tin (approx. 30x20cm) and line with greaseproof paper.

3 Put the butter and chocolate in a bowl, over a pan of simmering water, until they are melted.

4 Put all the dry ingredients into a bowl and mix.

5 Stir in the beaten eggs and then the chocolate and butter.

6 Pour into the baking tray and cook for 30 minutes. The brownies should be springy in the centre when you press lightly with your fingers.

7 Leave to cool. The brownies will rise in the oven and then go down when you take them out. Cut into squares when cool.

£1.23 TOTAL

EASE ★★★★☆

MAKES 12

PREP 40 MINS

COOK 8 MINS

V

GINGERBREAD MEN

You do NOT need a gingerbread man cutter, neither do you need to be an art student. Just draw your own gingerbread family on some paper, cut them out and then, when you have rolled out the dough, cut around them with a pointed knife.

If you do not have an icing bag, make one out of greaseproof paper. Take a square piece of greaseproof paper, make a cone and sellotape together. Put the icing inside and then snip off the tip of the cone. Screw the top of the cone around and squeeze. The icing should come out of the hole. Make sure the top end is screwed tight, or the icing will come out of the wrong end!

100g room temperature **butter**, measure using packet

1/2 mug **granulated sugar**

1 **egg**

2 tablespoons **golden syrup**

2 1/2 mugs **self-raising flour**

2 teaspoons **ground ginger**

2/3 mug **icing sugar**

2 tablespoons **water**

---

1 Grease a baking tray with some butter.

2 Put the butter and sugar in a bowl and beat together with a wooden spoon.

3 Add the egg and beat well. Add the golden syrup and beat again until smooth.

4 Add the flour and ground ginger and mix together with a metal spoon. The mixture will be quite stiff. Turn out onto a floured surface and knead together. Cover with cling film and leave 1 hour in the fridge.

5 Preheat the oven to 180°C fan/200°C/gas 6.

6 Place the dough on a floured surface and roll out. If you do not have a rolling pin, use a glass bottle. The dough should be about 1/2 cm thick. Place the ginger people templates on the dough and cut out with a pointed knife. Squash together the spare pieces, re-roll and cut out some more men.

7 Place the men on the baking tray and cook for 8 minutes. If you only have one tray, the dough is fine to wait until each batch is cooked.

8 Decorate if you wish. To make the icing, simply mix together the icing sugar and water.

£1.39
TOTAL

EASE
★★☆☆☆

MAKES
24

PREP
10 MINS

COOK
20 MINS

V

BASIC MUFFINS

Muffins are very easy and inexpensive to make. The flavourings can be varied according to what you may have in the cupboards.

3 mugs **self-raising flour**	1½ mugs **milk**
1 mug **brown sugar**	¾ mug **vegetable olive oil**
2 **eggs**, lightly beaten	24 **paper cake** or **muffin cases**

1 Preheat the oven to 180°C fan/200°C/gas 6.

2 Mix all the dry ingredients together, then add the 'wet ones'. They will be a bit lumpy and quite 'wet'.

3 If you do not have the individual cake tins, arrange as many cake papers as you can on a flat baking tray. If you use them double, they will hold their shape better. If you only have one baking tray, the mixture will be OK if you leave it in the bowl whilst the first batch cooks. Bake in the oven for 20 minutes. If you use the larger muffin cases, you will need to bake them for 25 minutes.

VARIATIONS

CHOCOLATE CHIP MUFFINS

Add two 100g packets of chocolate chips. Two different varieties work well; for example, white and milk, or plain chocolate. If you want double choc chip muffins, instead of the 3 mugs of flour, use 2⅔ flour and ⅓ mug drinking chocolate.

RASPBERRY MUFFINS

Add 300g of defrosted, frozen raspberries with the wet ingredients.

APPLE CINNAMON MUFFINS

Add 1 mug of finely chopped apple with the wet ingredients and 2 teaspoons ground cinnamon to the dry ingredients.

BANANA AND NUT MUFFINS

Add 1 mug of mashed, ripe banana + 1 mug of chopped nuts, (cashews, Brazils, pecans or walnuts) along with the wet ingredients.

£1.07 TOTAL

EASE
★★★☆☆

MAKES 12

PREP 10 MINS

COOK 15 MINS

V

SCONES

Scones are delicious with jam and cream, but you can make them with cheese and, depending on your taste, also eat them with jam, but not the cream! They are a fun, Sunday afternoon snack.

BASIC PLAIN SCONES

2 mugs **self-raising flour**

1/4 teaspoon **salt**

125g **butter**, measure using packet

1 **egg**, beaten + **milk** to make 2/3 of a mug

SAVOURY

Add 3/4 mug grated **Cheddar cheese** at step 3

SWEET

Add 1/3 mug **granulated sugar** and/or 1/2 mug **raisins** at step 3

1 Preheat the oven to 180°C fan/200°C/gas 6. Grease a flat baking tray.

2 Place flour and salt in a bowl. Chop the butter into small pieces, add to the flour and rub in with your fingers. Try not to work it too much, or for too long.

3 If you are making plain scones, go to step 4. If you are making either of the variations, add in the extra ingredients now and stir.

4 Add the egg and milk to the mixture and mix well with a knife. The mixture should be soft, but not sticky.

5 Turn out on to a floured surface and gently squash the mixture so that it is flat and about 5cm thick. Do not knead at this point. The less you handle the mixture the better. Use round cutters if you have them, but if not, just cut with a knife.

6 Place them on the tray, with a little space between them for them to rise and spread. Brush the top of the scones with some milk. Use your fingers if you do not have a brush.

7 Place in the oven for 15–20 minutes. They should rise a little and be brown on the top. If they spread into one another, don't worry, allow them to cool and you will be able to pull them apart.

SCAN ME

For a video tutorial on how to avoid over-beating cream

EASE
★★★★★

MAKES
18

PREP
30 MINS

COOL
2+ HRS

V

CHOCOLATE MINT SLICES

Add the water to the icing sugar gradually, as it can easily become too runny.

450g **hob nobs**

6 tablespoons **drinking chocolate**

250g **butter**, measure using packet

2 mugs **icing sugar**

4 tablespoons **water**

2 teaspoons **peppermint essence**

200g **dark chocolate**

1 Line a baking tray (approx. 30x20cm) with greaseproof paper.

2 Put the hob nobs in a plastic bag and bash with a rolling pin, or similar implement, until you have quite fine crumbs.

3 Stir in the drinking chocolate.

4 Gently melt the butter in a saucepan. Pour over the biscuits and mix well.

5 Pour into the tray and press down well. Leave in the fridge for 1 hour.

6 Mix together the icing sugar, peppermint essence and the water. The mixture should be very stiff. Spread over the chocolate biscuit base. Leave for 1 hour to set a little.

7 Gently melt the chocolate in a bowl over a pan of simmering water. Carefully spread the chocolate over the icing.

8 Leave in the fridge for 1 hour. When you cut into squares, heat the knife under the hot water tap and it will stop the chocolate from cracking too much.

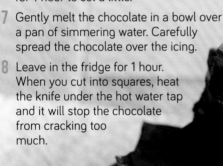

CHOCOLATE FRIDGE SLICES

£6.54 TOTAL

EASE ★★☆☆☆

MAKES 20

PREP 30 MINS

COOL 3 HRS

V

These would make really good presents if you put them in a little box, or make a fabric bag and tie with some ribbon. Think this suggestion could be limited to the girls, but you guys can take up the challenge and have a go!

150g **butter**, measure using packet

200g **white chocolate**

100g **dark chocolate**

300g **hob nobs**

1 teaspoon **vanilla extract**

250ml **crème fraîche**

1/2 x 250g pack **ready-to-eat dried apricots**, chopped

100g pack **roasted chopped hazelnuts**

1 Grease and line a baking tray tin (approx. 30x20cm).

2 Place the butter and chocolate in a bowl. Put over a pan of gently boiling water and allow to melt. Stir every now and then.

3 While the chocolate is melting, put the biscuits in a plastic bag and gently bash them with a rolling pin, or similar implement. Keep them fairly rustic, don't beat them to dust.

4 Once the chocolate has melted, take off the heat, add the vanilla, and stir well.

5 Add the crème fraîche and stir until it has melted into the chocolate.

6 Add the apricots and nuts and stir.

7 Put the biscuit crumbs into a larger bowl and add the chocolate mixture to them. The mixture will still be quite runny. Pour into the baking tray and place in the fridge for a minimum of 3 hours, preferably overnight.

8 Tip out onto a chopping board, take the greaseproof off the bottom and cut into slices. This recipe is quite rich, so don't make the slices too big. Keep in the fridge until needed.

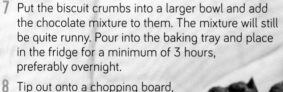

197

£3.88 TOTAL

EASE
★★★★★

SERVES
8

PREP
15 MINS

COOK
30 MINS

V

CHOCOLATE CAKE

If you regularly make cakes and cookies you might want to invest in some electric beaters. You can usually pick them up online for about £10. This would make an excellent birthday cake for your friends.

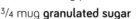

150g room temperature **butter**, measure using packet

³/₄ mug **granulated sugar**

3 **eggs**

1 mug **self-raising flour**

3 tablespoons **drinking chocolate**

1 tablespoon **water**

1 mug (300ml) **double cream**

140g bar **Dairy Milk**

1 **Flake** for the topping

1 Preheat the oven to 180°C/fan/200°C/gas 6.

2 Grease two 20cm round cake tins. Cut a round piece of greaseproof paper and put in the bottom of the cake tins.

3 Put the butter and sugar in a bowl. Beat well with a wooden spoon.

4 Add the eggs, one at a time, and beat well. The mixture should go quite pale.

5 Add the flour and drinking chocolate and fold in gently with a metal spoon. Do not beat the cake mixture at this stage. If the eggs used were small and the mixture is very stiff, add one tablespoon of water.

6 Pour the mixture into the tins and smooth out the top. Place in the oven for 25–30 minutes. When the cake is done, you should be able to gently press it in the centre and it will not leave an indentation, but rather 'bounce' back a little.

7 Leave the cake to cool.

8 Beat the cream until it goes nice and thick. Put one of the cakes up-side down on a plate and spread with the cream. Put the other cake, right way up, on top.

9 Melt a bar of Dairy Milk in a bowl over a pan of simmering water. Spread it over the top of the cake. Sprinkle a broken up Flake on top.

SCAN ME

Joy has done a video tutorial on how to melt chocolate.

£2.43 TOTAL

ASTRI'S APPLE CAKE

EASE
★★★☆☆

MAKES
16

PREP
20 MINS

COOK
25 MINS

V

These cakes can also be used as a dessert, if you serve them with cream or custard.

2 medium-sized **apples** (cooking apples are best, but you can use eating apples)

150g room temperature **butter**, measure using packet

3/4 mug **granulated sugar**

3 **eggs**

2 drops **vanilla essence** (optional)

1¹/2 mugs **self-raising flour**

3 tablespoons cold **water**

TOPPING

1/4 mug **granulated sugar**

1 teaspoon **cinnamon**

1 Preheat the oven to 180°C fan/200°C/gas 6. Grease and line a traybake tin (approx. 30x20cm).

2 Put the sugar and cinnamon in a mug and mix.

3 Peel and core the apples, cut into quarters, and slice each quarter lengthways again 3 or 4 times, making thin slivers of apple. Set aside.

4 Cream the butter and sugar together with a wooden spoon, until the mixture becomes soft and lightens in colour. Add the eggs and beat well. Add the vanilla essence.

5 Fold in the flour with a metal spoon. Do not beat. Add the water and stir gently. The mixture should still be quite stiff.

6 Turn into the baking tray and spread out evenly. Push the apple slices into the mix, distributing them as evenly as possible. Sprinkle the sugar and cinnamon evenly over the top.

7 Bake in the oven for 25 minutes. The top should be nicely brown.

8 Leave to cool and cut into slices.

SCAN ME

Everyone loves cake!
Joy has created more cake recipes for you to try.

£1.12 TOTAL

EASE
★★★★☆

MAKES
12

PREP
15 MINS

COOK
25 MINS

★★★
COOL
30 MINS
★★★

V

RED VELVET CUPCAKES

If you want nice, bright, red cupcakes, I would recommend using Dr. Oetteker's red food colouring.

50g **butter**, measure using packet

2/3 mug (150g) **caster sugar**

2 **eggs**

2 tablespoons **cocoa**

1 teaspoon **red food colouring**

1/2 teaspoon **vanilla extract**

2 tablespoons **cold water**

1 mug (200g) **self-raising flour**

1/2 teaspoon **bicarbonate of soda**

4 tablespoons **yogurt**

1 1/2 teaspoons **white wine vinegar**

ICING

1 2/3 mugs (250g) **icing sugar**

25g **butter**, measure using packet

100g **Philadelphia cream cheese**

small bar of **chocolate** (optional)

1 Preheat the oven to 160°C fan/180°C/gas 5. Put 12 bun cases into muffin trays.

2 Beat together the butter and sugar. Add the eggs, one at a time, beating between each egg.

3 Put the cocoa, food colouring, vanilla and water in a small bowl and mix. Add to the bowl and beat well.

4 Add the yogurt and fold in gently.

5 Mix together the flour and bicarbonate of soda. Add to the bowl and fold in gently. Add the vinegar and fold in.

6 Divide the mixture between the cases.

7 Bake in the oven for 25 minutes. Leave to cool for 30 minutes.

8 Beat together the icing ingredients and spread over the top of the cooled cakes.

9 If you want to get extra fancy, you can grate a little bit of chocolate over the top.

SCAN ME

For more cakes that will wow your friends.

DESSERTS

Think that making desserts is too difficult, but you have some friends around? Try some of these, just don't think about the calories!

RASPBERRY CHEESE CAKE

In order to get the cheesecake out of the tin, you will need to use a cake tin with a loose bottom. It is best to put a circle of greaseproof paper in the bottom. Once the cheesecake has set, loosen the side with a knife and place the loose-bottomed tin on a jam jar, or tin, and push the sides down.

£7.16 TOTAL

EASE ★★★★☆

SERVES 8

PREP 20 MINS

COOL 4 HRS

V

250g packet **digestive biscuits** or **hob nobs**

125g **butter**, measure using packet

1 mug (300ml) **double cream**

2 tablespoons **granulated sugar**

300g **Philadelphia cream cheese**

rind and juice of **lemon**

300g **fresh raspberries**

1 Put the biscuits into a plastic bag and crush them with a rolling pin, or similar implement (eg. tin of beans), until you have crumbs.

2 Melt the butter in a saucepan and add the crushed biscuit. Mix well.

3 Press the biscuit mixture into the bottom of a lined 20cm cake tin. If you do not have a cake tin, use a small casserole dish (don't try to get the cake out whole, just cut into pieces in the dish).

4 Beat the cream and sugar together with a whisk until it thickens. Stop beating once thickened, or it will turn to butter.

5 Gently fold in the cream cheese, grated lemon rind and juice. Pour on to the top of the biscuit mixture and gently spread out.

6 Leave to set in the fridge for 4 hours.

7 Decorate with the fruit (mash 100g into a sauce).

£0.24 /PERSON

EASE
★☆☆☆☆

SERVES
4

PREP
5 MINS

V

ICE CREAM AND CHOCOLATE SAUCE

This is a very quick and easy way to produce a dessert if you have friends around for a meal. Keep the sauce ingredients in your store cupboard and the ice cream in your freezer drawer.

125g **butter**, measure using packet

4 heaped tablespoons **granulated sugar** (brown or white)

3 heaped tablespoons **drinking chocolate**

2 tablespoons **milk** or **double cream**

ice cream

1 Place the butter, sugar and chocolate in a saucepan. Heat gently, stir well, and allow to simmer for 1 minute.

2 Add the milk, or cream, carefully, as it may spit at you! Simmer for another 1 minute, stirring all the time until smooth and thick.

3 Allow to cool slightly, before serving on top of the ice cream.

FRUIT FOOL

As the cream begins to thicken, be careful and beat more slowly, so that it does not turn into butter.

£1.47 /PERSON

EASE
★★★☆☆

SERVES 4

PREP 15 MINS

COOL 2 HRS

V

500g **mascarpone cheese**

1/2 mug (150 ml) **double cream**, whipped

6 tablespoons **icing sugar**

1 **lemon**, zest and juice

1/2 x 400g pack **frozen summer fruits**, defrosted

1 small **white chocolate bar**, grated

1 Mix together the mascarpone and the whipped, double cream and sugar. Add the lemon zest and juice and mix well.

2 Add the fruits (retain a few for decoration). Stir them in, trying not to completely break them up.

3 Spoon into individual dishes and leave in the fridge for 2 hours.

4 To serve, decorate the dishes with grated white chocolate and fruits.

£0.97 /PERSON

EASE
★☆☆☆☆

SERVES
2-3

PREP
15 MINS

V

FRUIT SALAD

This will not really last more than one day, as the fruit will begin to go brown. You can use a variety of fruits chosen from the list below:

apples	kiwi fruits	JUICE	QUICK JUICE OPTION
pears	pineapple	1 **lemon**	1/2 mug **pure fruit juice**
oranges	peaches	1 **orange**	
bananas	nectarines	1 tablespoon **sugar**	
seedless grapes	raspberries	1/4 mug **water**	
strawberries			

1 Cut the fruit into small pieces and mix together. If you use raspberries and strawberries, add them at the end, or they will break up in the mix and everything will be pink!

2 To make the fruit juice, squeeze the juices from the orange and lemon. Add the sugar and water and mix until the sugar dissolves. If you want to save time, just use half a mug of pure fruit juice instead.

3 Serve with whipped cream.

BANANA SPLIT

Make just before you serve, as the bananas will go brown if left for a long time.

£1.44 /PERSON

EASE
★☆☆☆☆

Chocolate Sauce (see p206)

1 **banana**

2 scoops **ice cream**

1 **Cadbury's Flake**

SERVES
1

PREP
5 MINS

V

---

1 Make the Chocolate Sauce.

2 Slice the banana in half lengthways and arrange on the plate or dish.

3 Place 2 scoops of ice cream on the plate, pour over the chocolate sauce and sprinkle the broken-up flake over the top.

OTHER IDEAS FOR 'EASY ICE CREAM' TYPE DESSERTS:

Sundaes made from layers of different flavours of ice cream, mixed with fresh or tinned fruit, chocolate or jam sponge rolls. You can decorate them with many varieties of sweets, e.g. M&M's, Maltesers, grated chocolate, cut up Mars bars/Snickers bars, nuts, etc. Just go to the chocolate and sweet counter at the supermarket and the world is your oyster!!

£0.31 /PERSON

EASE
★★☆☆☆

SERVES
1

PREP
5 MINS

V

FRIED BANANAS

You can cook maybe 3 bananas at a time in a frying pan. If you have more people, you will need to wash the pan between each batch, or the sauce will not work.

1 **banana**

25g **butter**, measure using packet

1 dessertspoon **granulated sugar**

¹/₄ teaspoon **cinnamon**

double cream, **crème fraîche**, **natural yogurt**, or **ice cream** to serve

1 Slice the banana in half, lengthways, and then cut each piece in half.

2 Melt the butter in the frying pan, add the sugar and cinnamon. Cook for 1 minute on a medium heat. The mixture should bubble a little.

3 Add the bananas to the pan and cook for a further minute on a medium heat. The butter and sugar should form a fudgy sauce.

4 Arrange the banana on a plate. Pour the sauce over the banana and add a good serving of cream, crème fraîche, yogurt or ice cream. You can get Greek yogurt with honey which works very well with the bananas.

MELT-IN-THE-MIDDLE CHOCOLATE PUDDING

You can serve it with cream, ice cream, crème fraîche or custard! It should have a crisp outside and a runny inside and is best served hot.

£0.71 /PERSON

EASE
★★★☆☆

SERVES 4

PREP 15 MINS

COOK 30 MINS

V

125g room temperature **butter**, measure using packet

³/₄ mug **soft brown sugar**

4 **eggs**, beaten

200g **dark chocolate**

1 teaspoon **vanilla extract**

½ mug **self-raising flour**

1 Preheat the oven to 180°C fan/200°C/gas 6. Grease a dish, it should be about 18x23cm and approximately 5cm deep. If you don't have one, use your casserole dish.

2 Mix the butter and sugar together and beat well with a wooden spoon. Add the eggs and beat well.

3 Melt the chocolate gently in a bowl over a pan of simmering water.

4 Once it is all melted, add to the sugar, butter and egg mixture, along with the vanilla extract. Mix well.

5 Add the flour and stir in with a metal spoon. Pour into the greased dish and cook for 25 minutes. The outside will be crisp and the inside runny.

£1.02 /PERSON

EASE
★★☆☆☆

SERVES 4-6

PREP 10 MINS

COOL 3 HRS

V

BOOZY CHOCOLATE TRIFLE

Raspberries are the best fruit to use, but you could also use apricots or pineapple. You will need to chop up larger fruits a little.

1 **chocolate Swiss roll**

1/4 mug **sherry**, **brandy**, **Tia Maria** or **Cointreau**

300g **frozen raspberries**, defrosted

1 mug (300ml) **double cream**

2 tablespoons **granulated sugar**

1 **Cadbury's Flake**

1 Slice the Swiss roll into 2cm pieces and arrange around the bottom of a large dish. A glass dish is preferable, but it will taste just as good in a casserole dish.

2 Pour the sherry/liquor evenly over the Swiss rolls.

3 Put the raspberries, and their juice, over the top.

4 Whip the cream and sugar with a whisk until thickened and spread over the top.

5 Decorate with a broken-up flake. Leave in the fridge for 2–3 hours until set.

£0.35 /PERSON

OREO CHEESECAKE

Deliciously monochrome!

EASE
★★★★☆

SERVES
12

PREP
20 MINS

COOL
3 HRS

V

300g **Oreo biscuits**
150g **butter**, measure using packet
1 mug (300ml) **double cream**

2 tablespoons **icing sugar**
340g **Philadelphia cream cheese**
rind and juice of a **lemon**

1 Grease a 20cm round cake tin (loose-bottomed if you have one). Cut a round piece of greaseproof paper and put in the bottom of the tin.

2 Put the Oreos in a plastic bag and bash them with a rolling pin, or can of beans, until you have something resembling breadcrumbs.

3 Melt the butter in a saucepan and mix with the crumbs.

4 Put two thirds of the biscuit mix in the bottom of the cake tin and press down evenly. Put in the fridge for 30 minutes.

5 Meanwhile, beat the cream in a mixing bowl, until thick, but not stiff.

6 Add the icing sugar, cream cheese, lemon juice and zest and gently mix together.

7 Pour over the biscuit mix in the cake tin and smooth out evenly.

8 Sprinkle the rest of the biscuit mixture over the top and gently press down. Leave in the fridge for 3 hours to set.

9 To remove the cheesecake from the tin, wet a tea towel with hot water and wrap around the cake tin to loosen the cheesecake. Balance the cake tin on a jar and gently slide the sides down to remove the outer ring of the tin.

SCAN ME

For more desserts that will wow your friends.

WEEKLY FOOD PLANNERS

BROKE MENU

MONDAY — SPAGHETTI PUTANESCA, SEE P54

TUESDAY — REST OF PUTANESCA

WEDNESDAY — HAM AND VEG SOUP, SEE P58

THURSDAY — EAT REST OF VEG SOUP

FRIDAY — CHICKPEA AND CHORIZO COUSCOUS, SEE P63

SATURDAY — EAT SECOND PORTION OF COUSCOUS

SUNDAY — EAT LAST OF COUSCOUS

CHECK CUPBOARDS FOR:

- GROUND CUMIN
- GROUND CORIANDER
- OLIVE OIL
- PAPRIKA
- VEG STOCK CUBES
- PLAIN FLOUR
- 2 CLOVES OF GARLIC

SHOPPING LIST

- BREAD
- CEREAL
- MILK
- SANDWICH FILLINGS
- 250g BUTTER
- 3 ONIONS
- 1 MEDIUM POTATO
- 100g CARROTS
- 1 STICK CELERY
- 2 TOMATOES
- 100g CHORIZO
- 1 TIN CHICKPEAS
- 1 TIN OF CHOPPED TOMATOES
- RED CHILLI
- 60g BLACK OLIVES
- 12g CAPERS
- 50g TIN ANCHOVIES
- 100g COUSCOUS
- 1 SLICE OF HAM (BUY EXTRA FOR SANDWICHES IF YOU LIKE)
- 40g FROZEN PEAS
- 200g SPAGHETTI

COST PER WEEK = £11.21

 = BREAKFAST AND LUNCH ITEMS. YOU CAN SWAP THESE FOR WHATEVER YOU WANT.

SCAN ME

DOWNLOAD OUR FREE APP to help plan your own menus

SHOPPING LIST

- BREAD
- MILK FOR CEREAL PLUS
  1/2 PINT FOR PASTA BAKE
- CEREAL
- SANDWICH FILLINGS
- 30g PLAIN YOGURT
- 40g CHEDDAR CHEESE
- HEAD OF BROCCOLI
- 300g CARROTS
- 750g POTATOES
- 8 SPRING ONIONS
- ROMAINE LETTUCE
- RED CHILLI
- 1 LEMON
- 1 APPLE
- 340g TIN SWEETCORN
- 150g FROZEN PEAS
- 2 CHICKEN BREASTS
- 2 COD STEAKS
- 1 WHOLE CHICKEN
- 1 CAN LAGER

TAKE-YOUR-TIME MENU

MONDAY SPICY CHICKEN MEATBALLS, SEE P129

TUESDAY EAT SECOND PORTION OF MEATBALLS

WEDNESDAY EAT LAST OF THE MEATBALLS

THURSDAY COD PASTA BAKE, SEE P132

FRIDAY REST OF PASTA BAKE

SATURDAY BEER CAN CHICKEN, SEE P134

SUNDAY SHARE LEFTOVERS OF CHICKEN WITH A FRIEND

CHECK CUPBOARDS FOR:

- DRIED PARSLEY
- DRIED ROSEMARY
- SMOKED PAPRIKA
- GRANULATED SUGAR
- CORNFLOUR
- PLAIN FLOUR
- OLIVE OIL
- SOY SAUCE
- TOMATO PURÉE
- WHITE WINE VINEGAR
- BASMATI RICE
- FUSILLI PASTA
- EGGS
- HONEY

COST PER WEEK = £19.57

STRAPPED-FOR-TIME MENU

MONDAY — 2 X QTY OF SPAG BOL, SEE P67

TUESDAY — SPAG BOL WITH BAKED POTATO

WEDNESDAY — SPAG BOL WITH RICE

THURSDAY — EAT THE LAST OF YOU SPAG BOL

FRIDAY — SMOKED MACKEREL PASTA SALAD, SEE P52

SATURDAY — EAT SECOND PORTION OF PASTA SALAD

SUNDAY — EAT LAST OF PASTA SALAD

SHOPPING LIST

- BREAD
- MILK
- CEREAL
- SANDWICH FILLINGS
- 2 ONIONS
- 200g MUSHROOMS
- 150g GREEN BEANS
- 2 SPRING ONIONS
- 1 LEMON
- 1/4 CUCUMBER
- 125g BUTTER
- 30ML CRÈME FRAÎCHE
- 500g BEEF MINCE
- 250g SMOKED MACKEREL
- 2 X TIN CHOPPED TOMATOES
- 1 LARGE POTATO (FOR YOUR BAKED POTATO)

CHECK CUPBOARDS FOR:

- OLIVE OIL
- TOMATOE PURÉE
- DRIED CHIVES
- DRIED MIXED HERBS
- BEEF STOCK CUBES
- FUSILLI PASTA
- 200g SPAGHETTI
- 4 CLOVES GARLIC
- MAYO
- RICE

COST PER WEEK = £14.44

SCAN ME

= BREAKFAST AND LUNCH ITEMS. YOU CAN SWAP THESE FOR WHATEVER YOU WANT.

DOWNLOAD OUR FREE APP to help plan your own menus

SHOPPING LIST

- WHOLEMEAL BREAD
- MILK
- CEREAL
- SANDWICH FILLINGS
- 150g BUTTER
- 7 EGGS (USE THE REST FOR LUNCHES, ETC)
- 100g CHEDDAR CHEESE
- 200g CASHEW NUTS
- 160g MUSHROOMS
- 3 ONIONS
- 380g POTATOES
- 1 RED ONION
- 2 RED PEPPERS
- 2 SPRING ONIONS
- 3 TOMATOES
- 2 COURGETTES
- 1 RED CHILLI
- 1 AVOCADO
- BAG OF SALAD LEAVES
- 400g TIN BLACK-EYED BEANS
- 295g TIN CONDENSED SOUP
- 4 TORTILLA WRAPS (USE THE REST FOR LUNCHES)
- 60 ML SOURED CREAM

MEAT-FREE MENU

MONDAY — CHEESE AND ONION ROSTI, SEE P62

TUESDAY — REST OF ROSTI

WEDNESDAY — CLASSIC NUT ROAST, SEE P119

THURSDAY — REST OF NUT ROAST

FRIDAY — SPICY VEG PASTA BAKE, SEE P120

SATURDAY — REST OF PASTA BAKE

SUNDAY — SHARE BREAKFAST BURRITOS WITH A FLATMATE, SEE P113

CHECK CUPBOARDS FOR:

- OLIVE OIL
- VEG STOCK CUBES
- 150g PASTA
- 2 CLOVES GARLIC
- DRIED BASIL
- DRIED MIXED HERBS
- MARMITE

COST PER WEEK = £18.42

INDEX

SUBSCRIBE

visit noshbooks.com/students

Get student recipes emailed to you every month.

THANKS...

This book would not have been possible without the help of many people. My husband Ron and my sons, Ben and Tim, have worked tirelessly to help me.

Thanks again to my very good friend, Fran, for her wonderful proof-reading and to Anna, for her help in the kitchen.

Many others came to collect and eat food on our photography days. Without them, much food would have been wasted, which is never a good thing!

Thanks to Tim and Ben's friends who have allowed us to use their faces for the front cover.

Josh Smith, Katy May, Josh Feben, Daniella Clements, Deb Smith, Andy Tiffen, Tommy Andrewartha, Phil Hatton, Felix Page, Jo Skinner, Joel Bennett, Michael Pearce, Rav Hayer, Patrick Wilson, Kat Thomas, Jan Moys, Calum Maciver, Rachel Tiffen, Marianne Matthews, Emma Page, Michelle Crispin, Gareth Matthews, Payin Swazey Attafuah, Mary-Jane Attafuah, Chester See, Erns Smith, Jon Herring, Charlie Gregson, Nathanael Bennett, Paul Cannon, James Malbon, Jess Whitbread, Tom Whitbread, Tim Crispin, Naomi Badu, Rach Clements, Hannah Clements, Naomi Clements, Nathaniel Ledwidge, Tekiva Ledwidge, Peter Kent, Beccy Catley, Matt Bentley, Nicola Goodwin, Leanne Clack, Trudy Willoughby, Cerys Duffty, Amy Banham-Hall, Jonathan Ingham, Tom Povey, Nicole May, Emily Malbon, Ross Macfarlane, Amy Macfarlane, Kirsty Macfarlane, Richard Wells, Juliet Adekambi, Simon William Burns, Sharon Makinde, Rachel Donley, Hannah Rich, Nathan Clements, Rachel Phillipps, Odele Caldecourt, Ben McCalla, Dan Richter, Jon Povey, Peter Goult, Connie Haywood, Jez Hill, Ed Gent, Jenny Copperwheat, Dan Copperwheat, Clarence Bissessar, Sarju Patel, Chris Low, Gabbie D'Mello, Esther Gore, Polly West, Kerry Cannon, Kirsty Crooks, Gareth Paton, Lizzie De Kraan, Jonathan Cannon, Matt Skinner, Luke Clements, Lizzie Fieldsend, Leland Fieldsend and Paul Summerville.

RECIPE COSTS

The recipe costs in this book are an average between Tesco and Sainsbury's at the time of writing. To keep the pricing relevant, we aim to update them each time we do a new print run. Latest costs are as at **March 2020**.

Published by: Intrade (GB) Ltd
Contact: us@noshbooks.com

ISBN: 9780993260988

Printed in China

1st Edition: 2002
2nd Edition: 2006
3rd Edition: 2011
4th Edition: 2013
5th Edition: 2017
6th Edition: August 2020

Author: Joy May
Recipe Development and Food Stylist: Tim May
Photographer and Designer: Ben May
Editor: Ron May
Proof-reader: Fran Maciver